PRAISE FOR

A FLY ROD OF YOUR OWN

"John Gierach is the American Turgenev—that is, if Turgenev had a sense of humor, fished like Lee Wulff, and was as wise as Marcus Aurelius. This means that no one is in Gierach's league when it comes to writing about trout fishing. *A Fly Rod of Your Own* makes you feel you are having a beer with your best friend, who is not only funny and companionable, but just great to hang out with. When it comes to fly fishing, Gierach is like a sex therapist. He has seen it all."

—Craig Nova, author of *All the Dead Yale Men*
and *The Constant Heart*

"Gierach's deceptively laconic prose masks an accomplished storyteller. . . . His alert and slightly off-kilter observations place him in the general neighborhood of Mark Twain and James Thurber."

—*Publishers Weekly*

"Full of thoughtful work on adventure fishing that will give you a case of the wonders. . . . *A Fly Rod of Your Own* is a lovely book, and if you're a Gierach fan, it's in your wheelhouse. If you haven't given the bard of Lyons, Colo., a shot yet, it's a good introduction to good writing and storytelling that will likely inspire you to do some fishing—and living—of your own."

—Chris Hunt, *Trout Unlimited*

"John Gierach is the patron saint of American fly-fishing. When days go extremely well on the river, I think of Gierach. When days go extremely badly, I think of Gierach."

—C. J. Box, #1 *New York Times* bestselling author of
Off the Grid

"In penning a recent tribute to a departed giant and fishing friend, Jim Harrison, I found that no one had better anticipated and articulated that loss than Jim himself. Gierach puts me in a similar position. Since no one writes of our sport more pleasingly, why not let John tell us what we love about it? 'We go into places like that to catch wild fish, and for more personal reasons that may be complicated or as simple as the urge to escape the present—which admittedly looks none too promising—into, if not the actual past, then at least the kind of timelessness where life still makes sense.' Amen, and thanks for a lifetime of pleasure and sense."

— David James Duncan, author of *The River Why*
and *The Brothers K*

"After 20 books on fly-fishing, you'd think John Gierach would run out of ways to say Me Fool Fish. But dive into *A Fly Rod of Your Own* and you'll find not just a host of enjoyably fresh takes on this magnificent obsession, but a fresh understanding of why Gierach is the bestselling fish-writer since Izaak Walton."

—James R. Babb, author of *Fish Won't Let Me Sleep*

"Informs, inspires, and entertains. . . . Gierach brings a skeptical, wry voice to the peril and promise of twenty-first-century fishing."

—*Booklist*

ALSO BY JOHN GIERACH

A FLY ROD OF YOUR OWN

JOHN GIERACH

Art by Glenn Wolff

Simon & Schuster Paperbacks
New York London Toronto Sydney New Delhi

Simon & Schuster Paperbacks
An Imprint of Simon & Schuster, Inc.
1230 Avenue of the Americas
New York, NY 10020

First Simon & Schuster paperback edition April 2018

SIMON & SCHUSTER and colophon are registered trademarks
of Simon & Schuster, Inc.

For information about special discounts for bulk purchases,
please contact Simon & Schuster Special Sales at 1-866-506-1949
or business@simonandschuster.com.

The Simon & Schuster Speakers Bureau can bring authors to your
live event. For more information or to book an event, contact the
Simon & Schuster Speakers Bureau at 1-866-248-3049
or visit our website at www.simonspeakers.com.

Manufactured in the United States of America

10 9 8 7 6 5 4

The Library of Congress has cataloged the hardcover edition as follows:

Names: Gierach, John, 1946- , author. | Wolff, Glenn, illustrator.
Title: A fly rod of your own / John Gierach ; art by Glenn Wolff.
Description: New York : Simon & Schuster, 2017.
Identifiers: LCCN 2016019507| ISBN 9781451618341 | ISBN 1451618344
Subjects: LCSH: Fly fishing.
Classification: LCC SH456 .G566 2017 | DDC 799.12/4--dc23
LC record available at https://lccn.loc.gov/2016019507

ISBN 978-1-4516-1834-1
ISBN 978-1-4516-1835-8 (pbk)
ISBN 978-1-4516-1836-5 (ebook)

Today is my sixty-fifth birthday. I am thinking how long it has taken me to comprehend fishing. To begin to see more than a submerged shadow of myself.

—JOHN N. COLE

CONTENTS

A FLY ROD OF
YOUR OWN

1.

A FLY ROD OF YOUR OWN

The goal of fly-fishing isn't just to catch fish, but to catch them with style. Or, to put it another way, no one ever sets out to be half-assed at anything. You'd recognize style when you saw it even if you didn't know the difference between a fly rod and a pogo stick. (If you're like me, it was the mere sight of a good fly-caster that finally sent you out shopping for a fly rod of your own.) Think of those fly-fishing films in which all the tailing loops and motorboat drifts ended up on the cutting room floor, leaving only the economy of effort and absence of theatrics you'd notice in anything that's done so well it looks easy. Filmmakers will tell you this ineffable quality is as difficult to capture as it is to find. After all, the first rule of style is: don't try to show off if you don't have the chops. And the second rule is: don't show off even if you do.

The fundamentals of fly-fishing take time and effort to learn, but once you get the hang of them you'll begin to have days when you fish beautifully. You won't be wrong if you feel that you've now entered the prime of your prime: the time when you're old enough to know what you're doing and young enough to do it without breaking a sweat. You can even be forgiven for thinking you've reached a pinnacle of competence and that from here on out it will always go this smoothly. It won't, but every day on the water is still a fresh start, and every fisherman goes fishing expecting the best, just as every painter sits down at his easel planning to produce nothing less than a masterpiece.

I'm not one of those natural-born fishermen—it didn't come easily, and I've always had to work at it—but I do have my moments. I've been fly-fishing for over forty years now, and even if I'm not the best wader, caster, fish spotter, or flytier, I've learned to work well within my limitations, like a three-legged dog that can still go for a nice, long walk. The effect is cumulative. You naturally bring everything you know to every day of fishing, and the more days you have under your belt, the more you bring. If nothing else, the fly rod that once seemed so strange and awkward will now be thoughtlessly familiar, and the push of current against your legs and the slippery, uneven bottom are no longer surprising.

Do you still remember the first time you waded into a river that tried to knock you down, and what a shock it was? I do, but only because I walk past the exact spot every few weeks and always shake my head over that dumb kid who tried to cross right there instead of thirty yards upstream where it's so much wider, shallower, and easier. I wasn't thinking clearly because I'd spotted a large trout rising in a side channel on the far side of the river—the biggest trout I'd ever seen there—and in my excitement I took the direct route. My father once told me never to take my eyes off my goal. He forgot to mention that I should also glance down at my feet from time to time to avoid falling on my face.

I didn't catch that fish, and never saw it again. I wonder now if I imagined it.

There are few broad strokes in fly-fishing. It's all specific details strung together in a precise order; too many details to think about, really, but over time you wear neural pathways and the process resolves itself into something like instinct. This happens gradually and comes from nothing but repetition. There are no shortcuts, and the hunt for shortcuts only distracts you from the business of letting the craft become second nature. Eventually you lose track of how little you think about it until someone asks you to teach them how to fly-fish and you *do* have to think about it. Why can't you explain it better than you do? Well, partly because you're not a casting instructor, but also because by now you've made hundreds of fine adjustments that you're no longer even aware of.

Still, some days you fish brilliantly and some days you don't, for reasons that are never clear. Often it has to do with the quality of your concentration. Fly-fishing isn't as hard as some make it out to be, but it does demand your full attention, so if you're worried that your investments are going south or that your wife is cheating on you, chances are you won't fish well. It sounds like heresy, but there really are days when you should have stayed home to take care of business instead of going fishing.

Other times it's as inexplicable as any other kind of off day. Yesterday you waded sure-footed through fast, waist-deep current, flicking accurate casts at will; today you're stumbly in six inches of water and your fly finds every twig and leaf in range. Maybe you should have checked your horoscope before leaving home.

Or maybe it's garden-variety stage fright. I almost always fish better with friends or when I'm alone and unobserved than when there are strangers around—especially strangers who stop to watch or, worse yet, train a camera on me. There are some casters who don't mind an audience and a few showboats who thrive on the attention, but most of us can do without unsolicited reviews.

Once I was steelhead fishing on the Sandy River in Oregon with a guide named Mark. It was my first trip with a two-handed rod, and I confessed to him that I was self-conscious about my spey casting. He just shrugged (guides can be ambivalent about a client's "feelings"). But then a little while later we came around a bend and saw a lone fisherman halfway down the run making one effortlessly perfect spey cast after another. Mark said, "Just stand here and stare at the guy for a few minutes and watch what happens." We did, and sure enough, as soon as he noticed us, he got flustered and pooched his next cast. Mark was just trying to show me that even those who know what they're doing can be ill at ease about their casting, but I immediately felt guilty about it. As a demonstration this was educational, but it was also pointlessly mean.

Years later I ran into Mark and told him my spey casting had improved since we'd fished together. He said, "Well, it would have had to."

For all the talk about innovation and the hot new fly patterns, rods, reels, lines, tactics, and destinations, most days fly-fishing simply consists of going through the motions, and there's nothing wrong with that. (Woody Allen said, "Eighty percent of success is just showing up.") The motions are often complex, subtle, and difficult to master, and they exist in the first place because they're known to work. Certain kinds of steelhead and salmon fishing are entirely mechanistic, designed to work the water in identical increments with a controlled swing so that every fish in a run will see your fly swimming at the same depth and speed. This kind of fishing usually goes best when it's done in a kind of trance, which is a good thing, because a trance is unavoidable. Trout fishing is sometimes more surgical, especially when you're casting to rising or visibly nymphing fish and the accuracy of your cast and the quality of the drift are crucial, although fishing is still an oddly passive-aggressive business that depends on the prey being the aggressor.

The particulars are always unique and sometimes surprising, but over time you see fewer and fewer things that you've never seen before, and what seems like inspiration often involves nothing more than going through a second or third set of motions, as in, "When all else fails, fish a beetle." On the other hand, genuine creativity breaks at least some rules; so if you're skunked and get a weird but interesting idea, try it. The worst that can happen is that you won't catch fish, which is what's happening anyway.

There's also the matter of being free and uncluttered in your fishing. This has never been easy for me, because I've always been a sucker for all the paraphernalia that bogs down the sport. Even as a boy the fishermen I admired weren't necessarily the ones who caught the most fish but the ones with the biggest and best-stocked tackle boxes—tray after tray of brightly colored plugs with stylized scales or frog spots and the blankly staring eyes of cartoon characters. I still have my father's old tackle box just as he left it the last time he went fishing nearly half a century ago, right down to the fossilized worm crud on some of the bait hooks. I take it down from the pantry shelf and open it every few years for sentimental reasons. This is now a private observance, because in the past I've shown it to collectors who all said it was a damned shame that the potentially valuable old lures weren't in mint condition in their original boxes, but had actually been *fished*.

But back to being lean and mean. Too much stuff leads to too much fumbling, both physical and mental, while clarity of intent can take the place of one hell of a lot of superfluous tackle. I'm able to

5

travel light on the familiar freestone creeks near home, where I fish comfortably with half a dozen flies and no more other odds and ends than will fit in a pants pocket. Part of this is the result of years of trial and error over wild fish that have to feed aggressively and opportunistically if they want to feed at all. The other part is the knowledge that most of these creeks are only minutes from home, and tomorrow is another day.

I can sometimes manage the same thing while steelheading, although all the spare Skagit and Scandi heads, cheaters, tips, and poly leaders that steelheaders now carry can make the handful of flies a moot point. I can even sometimes bring myself to go smallmouth bass fishing with two or three Whitlock's Swimming Frogs and some wire shock tippet so the occasional pike or musky doesn't bite off my expensive deer hair bugs. Still, I find it a constant struggle to live with the kind of simplicity that eliminates struggle. All I can do is keep reminding myself that Lee Wulff once said, "The last thing you should change is your fly," which is good advice that's easier to follow when you don't have five hundred flies to choose from.

But on unfamiliar rivers and those where the trout are known to be difficult, I still clank around with a waist pack containing no fewer than six fly boxes (seven if I bring streamers), plus spare leaders, multiple tippet spools, fly floatant, weight and strike indicators for nymphing, clippers, pliers, leader gauge, a line cleaning applicator that I never use but should, magnifier glasses for small flies, and a headlamp so I can find my way back to the pickup if I stay out past dark.

And that's pared down from when I wore a canvas vest with twelve pockets on the outside and eight more on the inside, plus two large, overlapping cargo pouches in the back. That was the last in a series of vests, each with more pockets than the previous one in case I needed them, which I somehow always did. (Nature abhors an empty pocket. So does the tackle industry.) But that vest began to produce a chronic ache between my shoulder blades that started in midafternoon and lasted until I finally shrugged the thing off at the end of the day. This was further aggravated by the large 35mm film camera I carried around my neck for a couple of decades in an unsuccessful attempt to be a fly-fishing photojournalist. There was an obvious rule here that I was finding it harder and harder to ignore—namely, that if your back hurts at the end of a day's fishing, you're carrying too much stuff.

I have an old friend who used to guide a highly technical tailwater out of a single small fly box, although I think he had a storage bin with more flies hidden under the driver's seat of his pickup. That's not as impressive as it sounds, since given time and attention, any river can be reduced to a single box, but it still makes the point. He said there's no need for redundancy because it's usually fly size, accurate casting, and a good drift that catch fish. He also said there's no reason to carry more than three or four of any one pattern, because if you burn through all of them, you're either having such a good day that you can afford to quit early or such a bad one that you should pack it in and try again tomorrow. He suggested that I had somehow confused flies with money in the bank, which is why I'll never feel I have enough.

Of course he's right, but I continue to collect flies—not to mention rods, reels, lines, and other assorted gizmos, as well as trips to new water—for the same reason everyone else does: because it's easier than becoming a better caster or lying on your belly on a riverbank for hours at a time to observe the behavior of insects and study the secret habits of fish. I'm talking about what you could call original research. My friend with the single fly box once said that most of what we all think we know about fly-fishing came from books, and that those books were written by people who learned most of what *they* knew from other books, and so on back for five centuries. That's not exactly right, but it's not entirely wrong, either. It explains why the best fishermen are the rare ones with all the time in the world on their hands or guides who spend their days watching the fish their clients are trying to catch.

Still, it's hard to resist tying new flies for a trip. Day-to-day life, with its death spiral of chores and errands, can make even a big fishing trip seem unreal right up until the moment you toss your duffel and rod case in the pickup and drive to the airport. But tying flies before a trip clears your mind and gives you something to do besides pacing, fretting, and packing more gear than you'll ever use.

And now and then it actually makes a difference. I once read that before negotiating a crucial contract or international treaty, you should research your adversaries to see what kind of food, wine, art, sports, music, and secret vices they like in order to get their distance and maybe sniff out a useful vulnerability. This also works with fish. Specialized fly patterns, especially the old classics, aren't just collections of pretty feathers or an homage to tradition; they amount to psychological profiles of the fish that have been biting them as if they couldn't help themselves for generations. Or so you assume, until you show up on a river with flies that were the gold standard there eight years ago only to have your young guide say, "Yeah, I think my dad used to fish these."

So it's possible to tie for weeks before a trip and still arrive without the hot new fly that hit the shelves about the time you were getting on the plane. These patterns pop up unpredictably throughout the season. A precious few—maybe one every few seasons—are genuine breakthroughs that are destined to last for a hundred years, but more often they're idle comments on existing traditions, or explorations of half-baked theories, or attempts to use new and interesting materials or impress other tiers, or the results of pointless fads like the craze in some pretentious restaurants of plopping fried eggs on everything or of calling sandwiches "paninis."

Flytiers are always looking for an edge and can't leave well enough alone for both practical and emotional reasons. They remind me of some poets I used to know who would write a poem every morning with their first cup of coffee while they were fresh from sleep and, as one of them put it, "still blessed with the different mind." In a way that was just an exercise in craft, but they all secretly envisioned publishing a critically acclaimed book called *Mornings* or *Caffeine* or maybe *Hangover* that would jump-start their careers.

All of that explains why I have something like twenty old fly boxes on a shelf in my office, all full of flies, some of which I haven't used or even seen in years but must have once believed in or I wouldn't have tied or bought them. For that matter, I still have my old hardback copy of Immanuel Kant's *Critique of Pure Reason*. It's a thin book but so dense it could shield you from radiation, and I promised myself back in college that I'd keep the thing until I could not only finish it but understand it. By now my philosophy degree has expired and I've abandoned the effort, but I keep the book out of stubbornness. Likewise, I could easily get rid of all those old flies, but it would be too much like sending a good dog to the pound because he's gotten too old to hunt. For that matter, I may find that I need some of them again. If not, they're at least souvenirs of trips that, for one reason or another, can never be repeated. And anyway, twenty fly boxes don't take up that much shelf space.

And then there's the inevitable question of motive. Sooner or later, everyone who writes about fishing gets around to talking about why they do it. It's an irresistible literary exercise that has produced great work like Robert Traver's "Testament of a Fisherman," which reads in part, "I fish . . . not because I regard fishing as being so terribly important but because I suspect that so many of the other concerns of men are equally unimportant." But even that masterpiece amounts to the answer to a question no one ever asks. In the real world, those who fish already get it, and those who don't couldn't care less. It's not exactly a secret society or anything; but really, if you want to talk about the trip of a lifetime to some remote river, don't waste your breath on someone who doesn't fish.

It does all seem to be about the trips, whether they're short or long, near or far, familiar or exotic, but in the long run, fly-fishing is less a series of discrete adventures than a continuous process that you learn to love for its own sake. It doesn't always pan out, and few of your successes will be as spectacularly memorable as your failures, but even the drudgery serves a useful purpose. A friend with a little ranch over on the west slope of the Rockies says he spends his days putting hay in one end of his horses and shoveling it up when it comes out the other end, but that this gives him tremendous satisfaction and teaches him things he couldn't learn any other way.

2.

RAINBOW AND WRONG WAY

Reuben didn't like the looks of the weather, and this is a man who's squinted appraisingly at plenty of threatening skies before climbing into the front seat of a floatplane. I don't know when he started flying, but he was a working pilot in the late 1980s when he flew for another place called Iliaska Lodge. That's when I fished there, and it's when we must have met for the first time. When this came up over dinner one night I was surprised that I didn't remember him, but Reuben wasn't surprised that he didn't remember me. To a bush pilot, fishermen are cargo; he sees hundreds in a season, and one is pretty much like the next. "And anyway," he said, "that was a quarter century ago. We're both older now, and our minds are shot."

The plan was to fly to the Togiak River for the day, then out to Rainbow Camp that afternoon for an overnight and another day on the water, and then back to the lodge again in time for dinner that evening. This is one of those outfits that keeps you jumping. Every day a different river with a different guide. The pace is brisk enough that anyone who thinks of fishing as just a relaxing diversion might be happier at home in a lawn chair casting off a dock.

Flying had been sketchy all week with off-and-on rain and a low ceiling, but that morning it was really socked in, and word by radio from the camp was that it was the same or worse out there. Reuben told my friend Doug and me to suit up, pack our waterproof boat bags, and be ready to go. We'd see how things looked in an hour or so. "Remember," he added philosophically, "it's better to be on the ground wishing you were in the air than in the air wishing you were on the ground."

As sometimes happens with backcountry aviation in Alaska, an hour or so stretched to all day, and Reuben finally came to get us late that afternoon. The weather still didn't look great and we'd missed out on the Togiak, but he said if he couldn't get through the mountains he might be able to skirt the coast of the Bering Sea out to Rainbow.

Sure enough, from the air the passes were forbidding gray walls, so we banked south to the coast and followed it over the water, where we could fly under the scud without hitting anything. It didn't seem to be raining, but drops of water streamed up the windshield.

We were in one of the cleanest de Havilland Beaver floatplanes I'd ever seen. This thing had been fully restored, including the cabin, which is unusual. These old planes are maintained with an eye to airworthiness, but inside they often feature loose rivets, paint worn to bare metal, and seats patched with duct tape. New upholstery is all but unheard of. The camp has three of these planes, identically painted in shades of beige, brown, and green with "Bristol Bay Lodge" written in small script behind the call letters. When they're lined up at the dock in the morning they look like the air force of a small island nation.

Reuben is the rare Alaskan bush pilot who claims not to care for these iconic aircraft. One night at dinner he mentioned that he was looking to buy his own plane, and I asked if he wanted a Beaver. Several lodges had closed during the recent Great Recession, and word was that with a glut of them on the market the prices had dropped by as much as six figures.

"God no," Reuben said. "Beavers are about nothing but power. They're good for getting airborne in a short distance with a heavy payload, but once they're up there, they don't really want to fly. You know all that fiddling I'm always doing with the controls? That's me just tryin' to keep the damned thing in the air."

We were flying low over the Bering Sea. To the north I could see maybe a quarter mile up a coastal plain veiled in clouds. I knew the mountains we'd originally planned to fly through weren't too far inland, but I couldn't see them. Below us were bare rocks covered with gulls and cormorants and choppy gray salt water that looked very cold. Reuben was busy fiddling with the controls. Keeping the damned thing in the air seemed like a real good plan.

We landed on a pond that looked about the size of a mud puddle from the air—exactly the kind of place a Beaver was made for. Doug and I piled out along with some fresh supplies for the camp. The old sports piled in along with an outboard motor that needed fixing. There were first impressions and quick handshakes all around. Dave, the cook, was a short, wide man with a black beard and a hint of Georgia drawl: good news for those who believe you should never eat at a place with a skinny cook. The guides, Tyler and Matt, were loose-limbed, bearded, scruffy, and young, with exposed skin like leather.

A month later I'd show a friend a photo of the three of us cradling a salmon I'd caught, and instead of complimenting me on the size and condition of the fish, he'd say, "Jeez, where'd you find those hippies?"

Reuben was back in the air in ten minutes, not wanting to dawdle in case the weather turned for the worse.

Before long we were in a johnboat motoring upstream to the confluence of the Negukthlik and Ungalikthluk Rivers, which the guides had understandably renamed Rainbow and Wrong Way. This was a quick errand before supper. We simply motored to a long pool where Matt and Tyler knew chum salmon would be rolling and caught a few. These were hard, muscular fish, but like all Pacific salmon they were there to spawn once and then die, and as soon as they hit fresh water they would begin to sour. They were silver when they had entered the river, but even close enough to the sea that you could smell salt in the air they were beginning to color up in dripping wax patterns of sickly greens and purples. Several years ago there was a move afoot to change the name of this fish to calico salmon, because it was thought that would sound more appealing to tourists than chum or "dog" salmon, as they're sometimes called. It never caught on.

As we neared camp on the way back, Matt's German shepherd, Kaiser, trotted down to the river and playfully hid behind the single tuft of tall grass on the bank with his ears clearly showing. The joke here was that when we walked past he *didn't* jump out at us, which is typical of this breed's dry sense of humor. You could say Kaiser was the camp's early bear warning system and not be wrong, but most days he was just uncomplicated company.

The camp was a collection of tents and tan-colored WeatherPorts (picture a cross between a wall tent and a Quonset hut). There was no light in the cook tent except for what little seeped through the canvas walls and the two small, translucent windows. A lantern would have required kerosene and a lightbulb would have burned gas in the generator, and there was no real reason to waste either. Even batteries for headlamps don't exactly grow on trees out here. Before my eyes got accustomed to it, I stepped on Kaiser, who is mostly black and continually underfoot.

Dinner was grilled king salmon and a Cajun rice dish with peas. Dave turned out to be one of those cooks who could do a lot with the little he had to work with, using a light touch and spices he'd brought from home. I've been introduced to any number of so-called chefs at fishing camps who turned out to be passable short-order cooks at best, but Dave was the opposite: a trained chef who was feeding fishermen in the Alaskan bush for private reasons while incessantly listening to Frank Sinatra on his iPod. Tyler said his girlfriend back home had suggested he lose a few pounds over the summer, but he hadn't been able to manage it. He shot Dave a look that seemed to fall halfway between blame and affection.

It didn't take a lot of imagination to see how things would go out here. These guys were in camp for months, and the interminable Arctic summer daylight would make time stand still. Days would revolve around meals and the daily weather call from the lodge to see about flying conditions: a mundane chore on which lives could conceivably depend. Wind speed would be an educated guess, but you'd get good at it with practice. Wind direction was easy, since the river was a compass needle running roughly north and south. There was a distinctly shaped four-hundred-foot-high hill a mile or so upstream, and how much of it you could see—if you could see it at all—would give you visibility and ceiling. If you were far wrong about any of this, none of the pilots would be shy about bringing it up.

Fishermen would arrive in twos and threes on a more or less regular rotation, adjusted for visual flight rules and the vicissitudes of weather. Dave would feed them, and in their excited preoccupation only a few would realize how good the food was. Tyler and Matt would try to get them into fish, answer their questions, point out sights that weren't always obvious in a barren landscape, and generally pretend that this was all just some people going fishing together instead of the job it was most days.

There'd be the whole range of people, from return clients who knew the score to fish counters with wild expectations to the couple who thought, *Last year we toured wineries; this year let's go to Alaska and learn to fly-fish.* And there'd be the inevitable dim bulbs. Tyler said one day he told a fisherman to mend his line upstream, and the guy asked, "Which direction is upstream?" There are infinite possible answers here, but the correct one is, "That would be to your left, sir."

Why people do this kind of work is an open question, and the answer is not the same for everyone. It's for the money in the strict sense that you wouldn't do it if they didn't pay you, but it's no surprise that the most authentic lives rarely pay off in terms of big bucks. Some are young and starry-eyed about life in the backcountry; others are older and realize that while your twenties and thirties can be about reinventing yourself, your forties and beyond are more about trying to make the best of who you've become.

Many of the people you meet in Alaska during the fishing season have entirely separate and sometimes vastly different lives elsewhere. That's a compelling idea—sort of like having a secret identity—but there can be reentry problems. A guide at Bristol Bay told me that when he goes home to his wife and daughter in the Midwest at the end of the season, he pussyfoots around for a while, acting more like a polite houseguest than a returning dad. It's not that his family isn't delighted to see him; it's just that while he's had his separate life, so have they, and they'll now have to get used to his presence the same way they got used to his absence months earlier.

The next morning the dusky light through what was beginning to seem like a perpetual overcast was exactly the same as it had been when I went to bed, and I had the sense that I'd only been down for a ten-minute nap. The only thing that was different was the river, which had swollen to three times its previous width and was now flowing in the opposite direction, accompanied by at least one seal. This tidal surge explained the enormous mud hook of an anchor in the johnboat that I'd thought was overkill when I tripped over it the day before. (First the anchor and then Kaiser; for some reason I was tripping over things.) It was raining just hard enough for me to put up the hood on my rain jacket. I got a cup of coffee from the cook tent and watched a bald eagle and two herring gulls loudly squabbling over a dead salmon until Dave called us for breakfast.

We motored through the rolling chums in the confluence pool and headed up the left fork looking for king salmon. It was late in the run and most of the fish would already be far upstream on the spawning beds, but some of the biggest kings like to sidle in fashionably late for the party, as if they don't want to betray their eagerness. It seemed worth a shot.

A lifetime of fishing runs through your mind when you look at new water. At first glance this could have been a small prairie river in the Mountain West, but it wasn't. If there were fish here at all—and there may not have been—they wouldn't be resident trout tucked against the banks or nosed into the riffles sipping mayflies. These would be ocean fish passing through on their final errand, and they'd be resting in the deep guts of the pools, sometimes unseen, other times rolling restlessly the way a dozing cat swishes its tail.

We worked half a dozen pools that all looked fishy and that had produced kings during the height of the run, snaking our hamster-sized flies on sink-tip lines into the depths where, we imagined, the salmon would only have to open their mouths. The weather was gray and borderline foul. The four-inch-long hot-pink-and-electric-blue Intruder fly Matt had given me was as gaudy and lively in the water as an alarmed squid. Everything seemed right. Lunchtime came and went. The confluence pool full of eager chums crossed my mind, but I wasn't about to succumb to temptation unless someone else mentioned it first, and maybe not even then. Above all else, a salmon fisherman is resolute—or so he tells himself.

It was late afternoon when I hooked a king in a trouty-looking pool with a defunct beaver hutch on the far bank. When I first set up, it felt as solid and unmovable as the sunken stump Matt had told me to watch out for in here, and for a split second my heart sank, but then the fish turned and ran.

King salmon are appallingly strong. It sounds overwrought to say that you can feel the ocean in a hooked salmon, but there's no other way to put it. When you hook a big one, all you can really do at first is hang on and trust that your knots won't fail and your reel won't seize up. The fish has your complete attention, and you believe you'll remember every second of the fight with unnatural clarity, right down to the pewter-colored sky and the cool drizzle on the backs of your hands. But memory survives as a series of snapshots, some of which get misplaced, so although I still clearly remember the fish in the net, I'm now no longer sure how it got there.

The fish turned out to be a dime-bright hen built like a little oil drum that had come back from years at sea well fed and without so much as a seal bite or a net scar. I was actually proud of her for having done so well for herself. We didn't have a scale, but Matt guessed the weight at thirty-two or thirty-three pounds. Tyler pointed out the sea lice around her anal fin and said, "This girl probably came in on the tide about the time we were having breakfast this morning." What a thought! I remembered a friend saying, "If it don't got salt water in its veins, it ain't a salmon," which pretty much says it all.

We'd seen some other fish rolling in this pool, and a few minutes later Doug was into one that took in deep water, turned at the surface in a fluid, silvery boil, and ran downstream, peeling off backing at an alarming rate. We followed in the boat until the fish wallowed briefly in a pool, and then followed on foot when it rolled and ran again. This was a strong, heavy fish, and even after a long fight covering an eighth of a mile of river, it bulldogged at the end. Doug didn't rush it, and Tyler stood poised with the long-handled net, waiting for his moment, both understanding that a wrong move here could blow the whole deal.

This was another bright hen in mint condition, almost a twin of mine, but noticeably heavier at thirty-five or thirty-six pounds. In the net it could have been mistaken for the chrome bumper off a 1952 Buick. Doug is a lifelong fisherman and a cool customer with a sly sense of irony. He's in the movie business now—a partner in the Fly Fishing Film Tour—but he started out as a numbers guy, and once told me he'd gone into accounting only for the glamour and the groupies. He'd played the fish calmly and patiently, with no visible sign of panic, but when he finally cradled this slab of a salmon all he could croak out was, "Holy crap!" Then his mouth continued to open and close rhythmically like a fish out of water, but nothing came out. This was his first time in Alaska and his first king salmon. It was also the only time I've ever seen him speechless.

I whipped out my digital camera for the hero shot to show the folks back home, but the battery was dead. No problem. Tyler dug his out, but it was dead, too. So was Matt's. What the fuck? Was there a mother ship hovering above us in the cloud cover, sending us back to the Stone Age with an electromagnetic pulse?

Doug's camera may have held a charge, but it was in the boat, which was out of sight around the bend upstream, and the fish was already getting her strength back. She'd be ready for release before anyone could run back and get it.

The four of us stood there with current whispering around our waders, reminding ourselves that the salmon is not the photo of the salmon, which will never quite stand up to the living memory anyway. The salmon is the salmon itself, here and gone so fleetingly that half an hour later you'll wonder if it was even real.

3.

THE SHORT LIST

A friend called from Texas. He said he was standing at the crest of a low, bare hill where he'd walked with his second cup of morning coffee to take in the view and get a cell phone signal. He'd driven down there from his place in western Colorado to deliver some horses, and he was happy for the work and happy for the change in weather five hundred miles to the south. "When your livelihood depends on horses," he said, "your two choices of working conditions are dust and mud, and after a couple of weeks of mud, dust starts to look pretty damned good."

Then he asked if I'd been getting out, meaning getting out fishing.

At my dentist's office I showed off a snapshot of a large king salmon I'd caught in Alaska since I'd seen him last, and in response he whipped out a photo of a twenty-three-inch brown trout he'd caught in the Madison River the previous fall. It was a fat, buttery-colored male with the kind of grotesque kype that makes non-fishermen ask, "What's wrong with his face?" The dentist's assistant stood by smiling patiently. I assumed she thought this was charming—or at least harmless.

At the post office another friend said that a few days earlier he'd been casting on the liquid end of a half-frozen reservoir nearby, hoping for nothing more than a few holdover stocked rainbows, when he hooked and landed an eight-pound lake trout, which around here is a pretty nice one. He said, "That's probably the biggest fish I'll catch this season, so it's all downhill from here," but he didn't really believe that. In fact, any fisherman would believe just the opposite.

So it was in the air.

The common redpolls that had shown up back in early winter were still hanging around the bird feeder when I heard my first red-winged blackbird. This was on a snowy, fifteen-degree morning, and the cheerful, summertime call sounded impossibly foreign, as if I'd just heard a toucan. I looked around for the blackbird, but all I could see were the ubiquitous juncos looking like little executioners in their black hoods. It seemed way too early for red-wings, and I wondered if I'd actually heard it after all. Maybe it was wishful thinking.

I *had* been getting out, though, mostly to a tailwater two and a half hours south. There was a time when I'd have said I knew this river well and I'd have been right, but since the 1970s it's gone through some kind of paroxysm every decade or so on average, after which it reinvents itself, after which I try to relearn it. Whirling disease, wildfires, flash floods, you name it. I once thought that if I fished this river for four decades, I'd know it inside out. It never occurred to me then that my hard-earned knowledge would expire like a driver's license every ten years.

Most recently, siltation from floods has turned the once-rocky riverbed into shifting aquatic sand dunes, and it's become more of a caddis river than the mayfly stream I was once so familiar with. So I make a habit of stopping at the local fly shop to ask the owner what the hot pattern is that week. At least, I used to ask the owner, before he started to show signs of the occupational disease known as "the red ass" and began staying home, leaving the shop to one of the off-duty guides. Never mind; the advice and the flies are still good, and my fly box continues to bristle with unfamiliar patterns.

One day I fished the river for hours without a bump—sticking it out as a matter of principle—before I found a little pod of risers and hooked and landed three trout in what turned out to be my last fifteen minutes on the water. I could see that the fish were coming to the surface, but I couldn't tell what they were eating and didn't dare wade close enough for a better look in the low, clear water. It was late in the day, and I understood this was my one fleeting shot, so I tried a nondescript size-22 parachute midge and it worked. Good thing, because the rise shut off like that, and I wouldn't have had time to stand around changing flies. After releasing the third trout I stopped to chip some frost from the guides, then looked back at the water and the fish were gone.

Another time I pounded the river all day with nymphs and caught only one fish, but it was a twenty-one-inch rainbow. This was one of those slow winter days when there was no reason to fish before ten in the morning or much after three in the afternoon, so I'd spent the same amount of time behind the wheel as I had on the water. I guess I was vaguely aware of the five-hour round-trip drive, the tank of gas I'd burned, and the day's worth of lost work in return for a single trout, but then, a wise fisherman never actually does the math.

We do have the advantage here in Colorado of having no closed fishing season, so you can be out with a fly rod any day you can find open water. At least I think that's an advantage. Some fly-fishers—maybe the smart ones—wait for the fishing to pick up with the pre-runoff hatches in April and May and spend what's left of winter on the usual grown-up obligations. But others fall victim to the circular logic stating that not going fishing on a day when you could have ruins you for anything else, so you might just as well go. There were days when I stopped to fill my Thermos on the way to the river and Mindy down at the coffee shop glanced out at the weather and asked, "You're going *today*?" Sometimes this made me feel like one crazy-tough hombre; other times I wondered why I hadn't slept in.

Of course, for much of the winter you're relegated to the tailwaters, because they're the only streams that aren't frozen. Tailwaters are what Thomas McGuane called "the great theme parks of American fly-fishing," with their more or less stable water temperatures and artificially inflated populations of insects and fish. They're irresistible for all kinds of reasons, but all those trout breed the peculiarly postmodern sense that anything short of a twenty-fish day is a bust, so when things are slow there's the temptation to lie about numbers or to vaguely allow that you're "getting your share."

Some fishermen get proprietary about these honey holes and consult websites daily to check on their wildly fluctuating stream flows. In these unenlightened times, dam releases have more to do with toilets flushing in the suburbs than with trout habitat, and this sad state of affairs can push some people up against the wall. Some years ago there was a rumor going around that the water board was bumping the spring flows on a local tailwater with an eye to keeping the rainbows from spawning. (Kill off the trout, this conspiracy theory went, and we won't have those pesky fly-fishermen looking over our shoulders anymore.) It sounded far-fetched, but after Watergate, Iran-Contra, *Bush v. Gore*, and NSA spying, anything now seems possible.

For a change of scene, some friends and I made the first trip of the new year to a favorite prairie lake. I left home before first light that morning and drove down the valley toward the state highway, squinting ahead into my high beams looking for the deer and elk that can pop out of the darkness like targets at a shooting gallery. I had a cup of coffee strong enough to wake the dead, but it hadn't taken effect yet, and I was cold and still ached for sleep. This has always been my dirty little secret: I love being up and out before dawn, but I hate like hell to get out of bed.

We were hoping for a half moon of open water to fish, but found the lake completely ice-free except for a fragile morning glaze around the shore. This lake is spring-fed, so the ice stays thin anyway, and a few days of halfhearted sun and a steady breeze had done the trick. We got there right at dawn, and although the air wasn't above freezing, there were already a few trout rising to midges. Could these tiny, delicate insects actually emerge and fly away when it was so cold? Probably not, which would explain why the fish were rolling with such lazy confidence to prey that couldn't possibly escape. We rigged up quickly, then sipped more coffee and warmed the sting out of our fingers before we started casting.

We'd timed this trip to slip in ahead of an approaching front to take advantage of the falling barometer that's supposed to make trout want to "eat everything in sight," as a friend who's prone to hyperbole says. I've never found that to be literally true, but trout do seem to like the cloudy skies that come with low pressure, and of course there's the self-fulfilling prophecy that allows you to do 70 percent of your fishing on a falling barometer, catch 70 percent of your fish, and conclude that it obviously works.

The front first showed itself as a dishwater-colored cloudbank oozing down from the Continental Divide and a nearly imperceptible, possibly imaginary lightening of the atmosphere. Trout rose steadily to midges—because of the falling barometric pressure or just because

25

the bugs were there and the fish were hungry—and we hooked and landed some of the chunky rainbows this lake is known for.

It wasn't until midafternoon that a gauze curtain of sleet started up the valley from the northwest. It hung there, two miles out, long enough for us to think maybe it was just a squall blowing by to the east, but then the breeze kicked up a notch and I began to feel cold pinpricks on the back of my neck. I hooked and landed a trout then that took my full attention for a few minutes, and the next time I looked, the silhouette of the foothills had vanished behind an opaque and utterly impersonal bank of sleet. The wind had clocked around so it was blowing straight down from the north, and it brought frozen drops hard enough that it was difficult to look right into it. Rocky Mountain weather is as dramatic as the landscape, but some storms seem particularly emphatic, and this looked like one that was capable of sustained seriousness. I considered the shelter of the pickup parked a quarter mile away and wondered how wet the bentonite of the two-track leading out of the valley would have to get before it became impassable even in four-wheel drive.

We zipped up our rain slickers and cast to trout rising in the narrow slick along the windward shore. By "cast" I mean we let our lines furl out in the wind until they straightened, and then placed the fly on the surface by lowering the rod tip. We got a few more trout on midges, but pretty soon it was pointless, and by five o'clock we were sitting in a Mexican restaurant in town. This was one of those joints where your enchiladas arrive so quickly you have to suspect frozen portions and a microwave, but after a cold day on the water you're too hungry to care.

Forty-eight hours later there was two feet of immaculate snow on the ground at the lower elevations and more than twice that amount in the high country to the west. And it was that dense, heavy, spring-like stuff that turns shrubs into moguls, builds precarious white hats on fence posts, and makes a snow shovel heavier than you care to lift too many times in a row. In Minnesota, where I grew up, they called this "heart-attack snow" because every winter it would spell the end for any number of elderly midwesterners. They'd trek out to shovel their driveways at age eighty-nine to avoid paying the neighbor kid a dollar and come back feetfirst. At the funerals people would say, "Wasn't that just like Bill?"

After the front moved through, I drove to the fly shop, where the storm had folks talking about the coming spring runoff. In just a few days the snowpack had gone from 77 percent of average (more than a little on the dry side) to 90 percent statewide and slightly over 100 percent in two of the eight major drainages. There were still half a dozen different ways the snow situation could turn out by spring, but one possibility was a normal spate followed by a perfect season, and that's the prediction everyone had settled on. The optimism at the shop was so palpable that I bought fresh tippet material—4X through 7X—and diligently wrote the date of purchase on each spool. I have a pathological fear of old tippet and live in terror that I'll break off a good fish because my 6X monofilament has gotten brittle with age.

Still, winter was beginning to wear thin for me. This didn't rise to the level of an existential crisis—it's just that back in the fall the first fires in the woodstove had been items of manly self-reliance, while five months later I was tired of carrying in armloads of wood. I still had the fishing duffel packed with a down jacket, a wool sweater, and the hat with fuzzy earflaps that makes me look like Elmer Fudd, but my private vision of fly-fishing was now tending more toward warm summer evenings and wet wading in vacant mountain creeks. On the other hand, the rest of the winter fishing was still there to do, and it would be a shame not to do it.

Everyone has his own take on this situation, and it's usually an unspoken assumption dating to childhood. For many in my genera-tion, fishing and hunting were understood at a cultural level almost from birth, but they were rarely discussed except in practical terms.

My uncle Leonard was a fisherman first and a hunter second, while Dad was a hunter who only fished between hunting seasons. But each of them thought you should be skilled at both; Dad as a matter of style and self-respect, Leonard as a way to avoid wasting bait and ammunition.

At an early age I could recite my favorite lures—the Daredevle, the Johnson Silver Minnow, and the Hula Popper—and I owned a shotgun and a rifle long before I traded my Schwinn for a Ford, but if you'd asked why I wanted to fish in the first place, I'd have been stumped. The stated goal of fishing and hunting was to bring home the bass, pike, bluegills, pheasants, and grouse that tasted so much better than anything Mom bought at the store, but there was also some other unspoken element to it. There was the aura of work about it, but there was none of the preening and posturing you now see from extreme-sport types. This was just a thing people did, and some things were harder than others. Of course, in those days I was mostly out with men who had recently saved the world for democracy in World War Two. These guys treated everything like a job and had a somewhat cavalier attitude about discomfort that boiled down to "Well, at least no one's shooting at us."

I remember ice fishing. It was a miserable business before the advent of power augers and heated shanties, when you spudded your hole by hand and sat out in the weather on an overturned bucket. I always suffered more from the cold than the grown-ups because I was deemed too young for the regular nips of peppermint schnapps that kept them either toasty or oblivious. Sometimes they brought me a Thermos of hot chocolate or, later, coffee, but an hour from the truck it would be lukewarm at best. I went because the grown-ups went, and I'd reached that point in life when I couldn't stand to be thought of as a boy for even one more day. It was always satisfying to bring home a stringer of delicious cold-water perch that had frozen into tortured postures in their death throes out on the ice, but I much preferred casting to lily pads in warm weather, although even in summer the fishing could be made hellish by mosquitoes and blackflies. Some days "trying a different spot" was just an excuse to start the outboard and outrun the bugs.

I especially remember going goose hunting for the first time. We walked out into snowy corn stubble with flashlights in a frigid predawn, picked our way through an elaborate set of silhouette decoys, and climbed into a five-foot-deep pit in the ground. I sat there shivering, breathing that fresh-grave smell, and thinking, *This is what it's like to be dead.* But an hour later I'd killed two geese with a shotgun that was once owned by my grandfather and felt like the kind of guy they'd someday write folk songs about.

On the way back from the fly shop I stopped at the hardware store for lightbulbs and batteries. I must have said something to set off the owner, because he launched into his stock lecture about the creepy intrusiveness of government, but then he seemed to remember how many times I'd heard this before, cut it short, and asked, "So, you been fishing?"

At home I read an e-mail from a friend who was holed up somewhere near Great Smoky Mountains National Park. He'd left a job in Florida and was fishing his way in the general direction of Michigan, following the retreat of winter north along the Appalachians in no particular hurry.

He said he'd caught some trout, broken a rod tip on a rhododendron bush, patched his waders with bathroom caulk and duct tape, and so on: a more or less typical report from a traveling fisherman. But eventually he'd gotten ahead of the weather and was currently waiting out a cold spell in a town where he'd found friends to party with and a barista who brewed coffee to his unusually high standards.

He wrote, "Coffee is one true friend, and a friend shared by many. It transcends language. Coffee, music, and fishing are transcendent. That's my short list."

4.

SNAKE RIVER

We drove north in August to fish the Snake River where it loops from Wyoming into Idaho over a thousand river miles upstream from its confluence with the Columbia. Now, everyone knows you don't need a reason to go fishing. In fact, reasons (as in ulterior motives) have a way of sullying what could have been an innocent impulse, but in this case Doug and I just wanted to get our friend Vince out fishing for a few days before he went in for his third hip replacement surgery. Until recently I'd known Vince as, among other things, a big guy who could grab my wading belt and drag me across currents that would have otherwise washed me downstream like so much driftwood. But in his late fifties, after years of weight lifting and other random feats of strength, near-suicidal downhill skiing, and four-wheeling extreme enough to bend the frames of Jeeps, his own undercarriage was finally shot and in need of a rebuild.

At this point he'd had both hips replaced by two different surgeons in the previous two years, and both surgeries had been botched. The second operation went okay except that the leg came out eleven millimeters too long: enough to induce a limp and twist his lower back painfully, even with multiple insoles stuffed uncomfortably into the shoe on the short side. And the first hip was a factory defect that never worked right. It not only popped and seized up like a worn-out bearing—keeping him from wading down anything much more demanding than a boat ramp—but it was also leaking chromium and cobalt into his system, causing a condition appropriately called "metallosis," so it had to be replaced. It was probably just as well, since the only way to fix the length discrepancy was to "go back in," as surgeons say, to lengthen the first hip so it matched the second, which entailed quartering him like an elk for the third time.

But when he called the first surgeon to talk about all this, he learned that the guy had walked into the mountains a month or so earlier and committed suicide with a shotgun blast to the chest, thereby permanently closing the complaint department. What followed was the usual shitstorm of doctors and lawyers: the two kinds of people everyone avoids until they need them.

If that sounds like too much information, you should have talked to Vince. Those operations had cost him time, frustration, discomfort, whatever faith he still had in the medical-industrial complex, and the better part of two fishing seasons, so it didn't take much encouragement for him to deliver the full play-by-play account. He understood that when people ask how you're doing they don't really want to hear about your operations in excruciating detail; it's just that this whole hip business had consumed his life, and he couldn't help himself. He'd even lurch to his computer and show you X-rays of his pelvis that made him look like a robot cobbled together with mismatched components. Put simply, the guy needed to go fishing.

We made the twelve-hour drive to Victor, Idaho, on a Monday, stopping often to let Vince get out and work his faulty joint back into place. Then early Tuesday we drove over Teton Pass into Jackson, Wyoming's, morning rush hour. Bumper-to-bumper traffic wasn't really on the itinerary, but we wanted to do Dam to Deadman—the signature Snake River float that passes right under the Cathedral Range—and the guides we'd hired worked out of a fly shop in downtown Jackson.

The day was unseasonably chilly, cloudy and rainy with a leaden sky reflected in the puddles in the parking lot. The weather felt more like October than August and would normally have been promising for trout fishing, but Snake River cutthroats don't care for gloomy days. They're friskier when it's warm and sunny, which makes them seem more carefree than the dour browns and rainbows that have taken over so much of their ancestral range and changed the character of the fishing.

While the guides got the boats in the water, I killed some time watching a kid of about twelve wearing comically oversized waders he was probably expected to grow into. He was making some high-quality dry-fly drifts without getting any takes, but without losing interest, either. At first I decided he'd grow up to be a good fisherman; then I realized he was *already* a good fisherman, just a little one.

When the kid finally reeled in and waded to the bank, I asked him how he'd done and what he was using. He said he hadn't had a touch and showed me a fly identical to the one I'd tied onto my own leader: a medium-sized stonefly sort of gizmo that the guy at the shop had hinted was all but a sure thing.

I said, "Well, good luck."

"Yeah," the kid replied, hitching up his drooping waders. "You, too."

That morning my guide, Ben, had taken in my worn, outdated tackle and the difference in our ages and decided I didn't need a lot of coaching, but when I missed a strike from a good-sized cutthroat fifty yards from the put-in, he may have begun to rethink that. I almost always pull the trigger too soon on my first fish because I'm more excited than I think I am, and then waste five minutes of fishing time feeling sorry for myself. But then a few minutes later I pulled it out by hooking and landing the next fish. It was smaller than the one I'd missed (what else is new?) but I felt as though I'd found my rhythm and the day had begun. From then until near dusk I'd have nothing to worry about and nothing to do but see if I could catch a few fish. The worst that could happen was that I'd have a pleasant float on one of the most beautiful rivers in the Rocky Mountains. This must be how it feels to be rich.

The conditions were weighted against us that day, but we teased up some fish to dry flies anyway. I imagined this was how it was for that kid back at the take-out: not so much that every fish hooked is a surprise, but that they all seem like a triumph of artistry over probability. And as a bonus, the corniest mountains in North America put on a show worthy of Ansel Adams, with black clouds pouring through the high passes like the weather at the end of the world. We ran into Doug and Vince in the other boat from time to time, and they were doing about the same: not a whole lot of fish and no real big ones, but they were all native Snake River cutthroats swimming in the water they'd evolved in and been named for. No complaints.

Vince was in the bow of the other skiff, sometimes standing, sometimes sitting, sometimes leaning heavily on the casting brace; whatever was easiest on his sore hip. He'd said that nothing lasted for long, but that if he kept shifting around, it was usually tolerable. It didn't matter, because he's a casting instructor who could probably pull off a decent throw while standing on his head, but even from a distance he looked uncomfortable and maybe a little discouraged. I know from experience that being hurt in your twenties or thirties can feel temporary and even sort of heroic, while later on, knowing now that physical insults are cumulative and that you'll never quite come back to 100 percent, you simply think, *Shit, I didn't see* that *coming*. So whenever I see a friend going through something like this—and it happens more often as we get older—I experience genuine empathy, but also hope that being secretly happy it's him and not me doesn't make me a bad person.

After breakfast the next morning Doug and I went to wade-fish the Teton River while Vince camped in the room to make phone calls to the opposing lawyers in the class-action lawsuit he was part of. They were trying the old legal maneuver of burying him in paperwork in hopes that he'd get frustrated and just go away, but they'd picked on the wrong guy. Vince has a reputation for being agreeable almost to a fault, but when pushed far enough he becomes coldly diligent and ever so slightly menacing. That morning he was armed with a pot of coffee, notebooks, pens, stacks of photocopies, and the knowledge that he wasn't fishing because wading a trout river on his bad hip had become too painful even to attempt. I could almost hear him on the phone saying, *So you want my entire medical history from birth? Okay, you got a pencil?*

Doug and I had never fished the Teton before, but we followed a hand-drawn map down a county road to a dirt turnout and a fence stile, and then continued on foot through a waist-deep bog and across a meadow to the river. It was wide and slow here in the open valley, with thick weeds growing to within inches of the surface. There were a few Pale Morning Dun mayflies drifting down the current in slow motion, and now and then one would vanish in the unhurried rise of a feeding trout. It was all as quiet and proper as dowagers in a garden sipping tea.

I'd seen this kind of thing before on large and small western rivers. What looks like a uniform sheet of current is actually hundreds of conflicting microcurrents that drag a fly line in all kinds of unpredictable and annoying ways. As for the rises, they reveal where a trout is at the moment, but fish feeding on a sparse hatch in slow water will sometimes cruise upstream, taking a fly here and a fly there until they reach some seemingly predetermined point where they drop back down and start again. This creates the illusion of more fish than there really are and presents an unknown number of invisible moving targets.

And we didn't have forever to figure this out. The morning was warm, calm, and summery, but yesterday's storm was still piled up in the Teton Range, and pieces of it were periodically tearing off and scudding across the valley, pushing cold wind and towing curtains of rain. It was only a matter of time before one of these squalls hit us and put off this halfhearted rise for good.

I'd bought three different Pale Morning Dun patterns at the fly shop that morning, each more insubstantial-looking than the last, and I picked one with either the confidence that comes from years of experience or the kind of wishful thinking that gets a fisherman through the day. A little over an hour later, Doug had hooked one fish that stayed on briefly and then spit the hook, and I'd stuck one that took me into the weeds and broke off. Then the wind and rain hit and the rise was over, just like that. It was actually a relief, as if I'd been four shots into a game of 8-ball only to realize I was being hustled, but then the bar closed before the game ended, so the bet was off and my pride was technically intact.

By that afternoon, what began as an isolated shower had developed into a steady rain, and we fished a few miles downstream where the river narrowed into riffly, willow-lined meanders. The browns and rainbows here liked this gloomy weather, and by fishing blind with dry flies, we easily caught more than enough fat little trout to pull out the day.

Back at the room, Vince asked, "So, how'd it go?"

I shrugged and said, "Well, we caught some fish, but I'd much rather have spent the day talking to lawyers."

Thursday morning we met our guides at the fly shop in Victor, which was the usual midseason morning madhouse. Dozens of pickups with boat trailers were parked in the lot at odd angles, and dozens more guides and sports were milling around in the shop, in the parking lot, and across the street at a strategically located coffee kiosk. I went inside to buy some flies and say hello to the shop dog I'd made friends with the day before. I was told he'd been petted so many times already that morning that he'd finally gone into the office to lie down.

We were floating what they call the South Fork, which isn't a fork at all but the main branch of the Snake below Palisades, the second of the sixteen dams that amount to choke collars on this big, once-wild river whose waters are coveted by advocates for potatoes, electricity, and trout, more or less in that order. Vince and I were in one boat and Doug and his friend Melanie were in the other. Doug is on the board of directors of Casting 4 a Cure, an event that's held in and around Victor every year to benefit Rett syndrome research, so he knows everyone in the area in the fishing business, plus a whole lot of others, including Melanie. She's the assistant manager of the lodge where the event is held, and she took the day off when she learned there'd be an empty seat in one of the boats.

Our guide was yet another friend of Doug's named George, and I liked him immediately. He was twenty-five years old, happily married with a three-year-old daughter, and said all he'd ever wanted was to be a fishing guide. In fact, he'd wanted it so badly that in his teens he lied about his age to get his first guiding job. (Well, he didn't actually lie; no one asked his age, and he didn't volunteer it.) This is precisely the guy you want on the oars when you're launching a small boat on a big river: young and eager, but seasoned and with the easy confidence of a man who's achieved his goal. I remembered a similar feeling from when I was sixteen and all I'd wanted from my own life was to get a driver's license and lose my virginity. (This was the era of drive-in movies, and I had correctly surmised that the former could lead to the latter.) I may have dimly understood that in the fullness of time I'd aspire to something more, but in that moment there was no way things could have gotten any better.

We put in at Spring Creek and started out pounding the banks with wind-resistant floating stonefly patterns that went by our ears on the forward cast with a sound like paper tearing. The fish were holding so tight to the bank that you had to aim for that inch-wide tongue of current right against the grass. Two or three inches would sometimes be enough for an eager trout—usually a smaller one—but at six inches out you might as well have been fishing open water.

Banging banks is an instinctive skill. The boat and the current are traveling at different speeds, and your targets are advancing and receding unpredictably while canopies of overhanging willows appear like premonitions in your peripheral vision. It takes a feel for spatial relationships and timing, as well as some low-level athleticism with the fly rod. The only analogy I can think of is my father's description of shooting at enemy planes from the rear turret of a torpedo bomber during World War Two. No two setups were the same and everything was moving except the sky, but if you knew what you were doing you could still draw a sinuous line from point A to point B with .50-caliber tracers. That was the only war story he ever told that involved actual gunplay, and then only as an example of the technique of marksmanship.

Things started slowly, but the trout got grabbier as the morning sun warmed the river, although they still stayed tucked against their banks as though they were hiding from fishermen, as they probably were. This is a hard-fished river—the shop in Victor alone fields upward of thirty boats a day—and everyone pounds the banks in the mornings. But as George pointed out, even the best caster can hit only one out of every three or four good lies as the boat drifts past, and many of these fishermen *aren't* the best casters. He didn't seem to mean that unkindly; it was just the observation of a hardworking guide.

We caught trout on stoneflies in fits and starts all morning, periodically switching out one fly pattern for another as the ones we'd been using went cold. No one knows why this happens—some think it's a collective mood shift among the trout, others believe it's the quality and direction of the light hitting the water—but sometimes the pattern that's been working for the last forty-five minutes abruptly wears out its welcome and you have to change the game. You're looking for something identifiably similar but noticeably different, and luckily there are as many stonefly patterns in the Mountain West as there are flytiers who have put their minds to the problem. This is one reason why the fly boxes of twenty years ago would fit in your hip pocket, while many of those made today are the size of briefcases.

But George had worked out a neat system for keeping the number of flies he carried to a minimum. All his stonefly patterns, regardless of size or configuration, were tied with light cream-colored bodies that he would then tint with various waterproof Magic Markers, mixing lighter colors to get darker ones until eventually the body of the fly was black. He said he had to do this entirely on faith because he was color-blind.

George had timed the float so that we'd come into a stretch of shelving riffles just as a Pale Morning Dun hatch began late in the morning. We anchored out and caught cutthroats on light leaders and small dry flies, switching one pattern for another to find the killer fly and then switching again when the fish got suspicious. In the shallow, clear water and bright sun we could see the rising fish clearly and picked out the biggest ones as if we were window-shopping.

These were long, wide riffles, and we were among a dozen other boats anchored at a respectful distance from one another, including the one that held Doug and Melanie. The day had turned warm by then, and Melanie was now fishing in short shorts and a halter top. It was fun watching fishermen in the other dories gawking openly while big cutthroats ate their flies and then spit them back out again with impunity.

After the hatch petered out we went back to banging the banks with stoneflies, and by late afternoon we'd caught so many trout that Vince and I each offered to take the oars for a while so George could fish, but he declined with the kind of rote professionalism you often hear from guides. "I just like to see the eat," he said. "I don't have to be holding the rod." This is undoubtedly true, but it can also be a polite way of saying "I don't let strangers row my boat."

It began to rain again late in the day, but by then we were far enough downriver to have gotten past most of the cutthroats and into the browns and rainbows that like that kind of weather, so it continued to be the kind of charmed day when you can't keep 'em off the hook. I got my last fish while I was reeling in after my last cast.

We did the full thirty-four miles from Spring Creek to Twin Bridges that day, motoring through the last few miles of frog water with a little outboard and watching bald eagles perched on volcanic cliffs that looked like melted chocolate. We'd spent a good ten or eleven hours in the boat, and I should have asked Vince how his hip was doing, but I forgot all about it. With any luck, so did he.

We drove home on Friday, and Vince went in for the operation on Monday morning. The surgeon said the procedure went perfectly, but then, he wasn't the one who had to recover from it. For his part, Vince was sore and woozy, but he said the first time he stood up he was happy to find that both his legs were the same length.

Three weeks later we went fishing again.

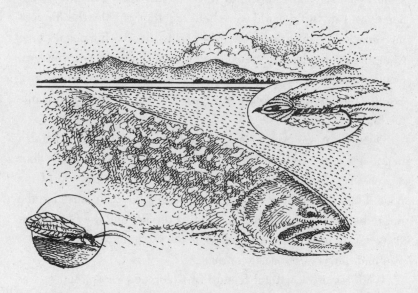

5.

FIREPROOF

It was the kind of bone-dry, ninety-eight-degree day that makes the enameled blue Colorado sky feel like an anvil on your head. It hadn't rained in a month and everything was wilted, from the junipers and cottonwoods along the gulch to the sleeping cats draped over the porch railing like dishrags. And taking up most of the northern horizon was the immense plume of gray smoke from the High Park fire with slurry bombers swarming it like flies.

I was packed for a fishing trip and was wondering whether I

should cancel. Things do tend to go south when I'm away from home, as if my little world were held together only by the force of my presence. There have been blizzards, floods, hurricane-force Chinook winds, downed trees, troublesome bears, power outages, plugged toilets, you name it, while I've been gone. Susan once asked, "Why is it that you're always off fishing when the shit hits the fan?"

Once there was even a fire. I came home from British Columbia to find a twenty-acre fan-shaped burn mark stretching from the floor of the valley to the natural firebreak of rim rock at the top of the ridge. I heard the whole story—the idiot neighbor who started it; the run-in between residents ineptly fighting the fire and the Forest Service crew—but by the time I got home the excitement was long since over and things were back to normal.

Wildfires are a natural feature of Colorado's ecosystem, and as long as we've lived in this valley I can't remember a summer when we couldn't see and sometimes smell the smoke—and once the actual flames—from one fire or another. Everyone we know has an evacuation plan stuck to their refrigerator, including a detailed list of items to take. Fire causes people to lose sight of what's useful, and there are stories of otherwise rational folks fleeing their homes with nothing but a handful of steak knives and a duck decoy.

And High Park was a nasty one: forty-six thousand acres at the time and spreading by the hour. It was 10 percent contained (or 90 percent *un*contained), and the hot, dry conditions had turned the woods to kindling. More to the point, it was only twenty miles north of the house. A firefighter friend said he couldn't imagine even a big one burning that far at right angles to a prevailing westerly wind, but then carefully added that he wasn't offering a guarantee.

I asked Susan if she thought I should stay home, and she said no. In the twenty-three years we've lived together, she has never so much as hinted that I not go fishing (a working definition of "true love"), but she did ask me to get my stuff together in case things changed and she had to evacuate.

It didn't take long. There were the usual bankbooks, insurance policies, and other important papers, a stack of fly rods, a milk crate full of reels and fly boxes, and a framed photo of my late father taken when he was a tail gunner during World War Two. It was absolutely everything I would need to start over, and it made a disappointingly unimpressive little pile. The next morning I drove to the airport and flew to Maine.

I met Carter Davidson at the baggage claim and we drove north toward Bethel, Maine, and the Androscoggin River, where we would rendezvous with my writer and editor friend Jim Babb and Carter's guide friend Rick Estes. The weather out east had also been in the nineties, but by the time I got there the hot spell had broken, with low clouds, rain, and highs in the sixties. I can't tell you how good it felt to zip up a fleece vest after weeks of Colorado's apocalyptic heat wave. It does get really warm in the American Southwest and you learn to live with it, but when it's too hot for too long I begin to act like an old pickup I used to own that would stall, vapor lock, and refuse to restart until it cooled off.

I know Carter as a documentary filmmaker and fishing guide: two professions that have bred the kind of inventive optimism that lets him regularly make something worthwhile out of things as they are. We stopped on the way to the river to pick up his drift boat at a friend's house. It was a handsome wooden dory that he'd built a few winters earlier, and as we trailered it up he pointed out some flaws in its construction that only the builder would see. This is akin to saving a life with a delicate operation and then, because you're a perfectionist, apologizing because the stitches closing the incision could have been straighter.

The Androscoggin is a big, mostly placid river surrounded by the kind of lush, juicy forest that in my current state of mind struck me as almost fireproof. The first day out we drifted into a mating flight

43

of alderflies. They looked like beige snow swirling in the crowns of the black spruce trees before they dropped down to the surface to lay their eggs and get eaten by trout. We anchored out and caught some fat little browns and rainbows, but the one bigger trout rising off by himself refused everything I threw at him and finally went away. I told myself it was an impossible drift.

The next day was dark and rainy and the river farther downstream seemed dead until we started to pick up fish in a bankside run below a tributary stream. These were the same sort of stocky, workmanlike trout, and it seemed as though every fish within a mile of river was crammed into this narrow seam. Jim and I landed a dozen each on small wet flies before we began to suspect an unfair advantage, so we beached the boat and took some water temperatures. The river had warmed up during the recent hot spell, and even with the cooler weather it was still near seventy degrees, while the creek was closer to sixty. Those trout had crowded into the mouth of that stream trying to cool off.

Later that day we fished through an hour-long downpour that may have chilled the water a few degrees, and Jim landed two big rainbows on nymphs in a hundred yards of river while I somehow stumbled onto the perfect drift for chubs.

The next day Jim, Carter, and I would be driving to the Rapid River, where there was no landline or cell phone reception, so that evening I called home to check on things. The temperature in Colorado that day had hit 102 degrees with a humidity of 7 percent. The High Park fire had grown to fifty-four thousand acres—still mostly out of control—and the evacuation center near the town of Laporte had itself been evacuated because of smoke.

"What's it like there?" Susan asked.

"It's raining and in the fifties," I said, not quite managing to sound matter-of-fact. I was trying to muster at least a mild case of survivor's guilt, but was overcome by selfish animal comfort.

"I'll bet that feels good," she said.

"Yes, it does," I admitted.

The Rapid River owes its fame to two women. One was Louise Dickinson Rich, author of dozens of books but best known for her 1942 bestseller *We Took to the Woods*, which introduced America to the laconic rural Mainer many think of as a stock fictional character until they meet one in the flesh. The other was Carrie Stevens, the milliner turned flytier who invented no fewer than twenty now-classic streamer patterns, including the beautiful Gray Ghost that has survived ninety years of changing fashions better than blue jeans. The Rapid also happens to be one of the last rivers in Maine where you can catch a five-pound brook trout—which doesn't mean you will.

We splashed a mile or so up a dirt road full of puddles to Rich's old summer house and walked around to the kitchen door to check in with Aldro French, who now runs the place as a combination historic site and fish camp. French is a large, barrel-chested man with a shock of white hair that hangs down to his shoulders. On a chilly day he wore a faded sweatshirt with the sleeves cut off, shorts, and flip-flops. He was the type who could be either younger or older than he looks, although something in his manner makes you suspect older.

French ushered us into the big, cluttered New England kitchen, served us stunningly strong warmed-over coffee, and delivered a monologue that went from martinis to Mount Rushmore to coffee cups to salmon fishing to crank telephones to dogs to magazines and so on without the benefit of transition. Later Jim suggested that the man might be a little "woods queer": an old Maine term for those who have grown peculiar from spending too much time alone in the bush. When the subject of Louise Dickinson Rich pilgrims came up, French said, "In fact, I got a bunch of old ladies coming in to-morrow." Then he added, apparently to himself, "Hell, at my age I don't know who I can call an 'old lady' anymore." Later Jim said that a common symptom of woods queerness is doing your stream-of-consciousness thinking out loud.

We started at Lower Dam, where the old log sluices and stone riprap churned the river into incomprehensible currents. Jim and I spread out along the near bank fishing dry flies in the braided pocket water. Carter had perched on a rock where he could reach a main current tongue with a streamer. Farther out, some fishermen had climbed down the aprons of the dam to swing streamers as fishermen have done since Carrie Stevens fished the prototype of the Gray Ghost on the Rapid and caught the six-pound, thirteen-ounce brook trout that came in second in the 1924 *Field & Stream* fishing contest.

The story goes that the first Gray Ghost was plain and simple—just white bucktail and dun saddles on a bare hook—but Stevens, who knew about exotic feathers from making ladies' hats and about fishermen from living in Maine, later prettied it up with orange silk floss, silver tinsel, peacock herl, silver pheasant, and jungle cock to make it more saleable, thereby inventing what we now know as the New England–style streamer.

The rest is the history some fly-fishers no longer seem all that interested in, although to others the angling past, with its big fish, fancy flies, and dowdy characters, is still surrounded by an amber glow, as if it were backlit by kerosene lamps. Things really were different then. Carrie Stevens was married to a guide and she did fish, but she wasn't what some bloggers would now call a "chick in waders." In the black-and-white photos I've seen, she's in a proper dress and pearls and looks like your grandma on her way to church.

The Rapid's legendary big brook trout were scarce that day—it hasn't been like the 1920s since the 1920s—but we got a few chubby little ones as well as some landlocked salmon that were as exotic to me as peacock bass. You couldn't ask for more from a game fish than you get from a landlocked salmon. They're bright and pretty, they feed freely without being pushovers, and once hooked, they spend as much time in the air as in the water. They're like bonefish in that you never get past thinking they should be bigger than they turn out to be based on the fight they put up. Jim got one below the ruined pilings of Middle Dam that, before it was all over, had tangled his two-nymph-and-indicator rig beyond repair and tied an overhand knot in his fly line.

A few days later at Bosebuck Mountain Camps, I was introduced to the owners, Mike and Wendy Yates. When Wendy learned I was from Colorado, she said she'd just heard on the radio that a big fire out there had blown up and there were a bunch of fresh evacuations. I asked where, but she didn't remember. There was no cell phone reception there, either, so she let me call home on their landline.

Susan said High Park had grown past eighty thousand acres but was now burning northwest, away from the house and into largely uninhabited state forest along the Cache la Poudre River. The fire that had made the national news was Waldo Canyon, a new one a hundred miles to the south. Our friends Ed and Jana were among those who'd been evacuated from Manitou Springs, and the last Susan heard, they'd gotten out okay and were on their way to stay with friends. No word since then.

"What's it like there?" I asked.

"Hot. In the hundreds. And smoky."

She didn't ask what it was like in Maine, and I didn't volunteer that the rain had stopped, the skies had cleared, and it was warming up. Midseventies with a pleasant breeze was not what she'd consider "warm." I was still on the phone when Wendy came back in and gave me a questioning look. When I answered with a thumbs-up, she flashed me a smile I can only describe as genuine.

The only rule I was aware of at the lodge was that you showed up on time when the bell rang for dinner, and that evening everyone did. I could see that Wendy was the kind of small, good-natured woman whom men instinctively obey on the rare occasions when she puts her foot down.

The dining room was café-sized and pine-paneled, with plank tables and plain, straight-backed chairs. Along one wall was a line of mounted white-tailed deer heads looking as solemn as Supreme Court justices. The place was less than half full because the good spring fishing was winding down into the hot, buggy summer, and they wouldn't see crowds of fishermen again till fall. Soon the cabins would begin to fill up with family vacationers, which Mike wasn't looking forward to. They were fine for the most part, he said, but after a few days they'd run short on activities and begin to find things for him to fix: a sticking door, a loose porch step, a rattling doorknob. Mike preferred fishermen, at least partly because they were gone all day.

We met up with Rick Estes again (he guides at the lodge) and fished the Magalloway. This is a pretty, tea-colored river flowing through mixed coniferous and deciduous woods, and we fished it with sink-tips and streamers because the brook trout and salmon wouldn't be looking up in the warm, bright weather.

I opened my streamer box and asked Rick if anything looked good among the large, drab western flies with big heads and staring dumbbell eyes. He glanced at it and scowled almost imperceptibly, then opened his own box and offered me a small Gray Ghost. Rick is a broad-shouldered, rough-hewn guy. In a diner filled with loggers and truck drivers, you'd easily pick out Carter as a fishing guide, but you might overlook Rick. He's a policeman turned game warden turned guide and exudes the air of someone who's seen it all (including a reported UFO crash) and hasn't been surprised by any of it in quite some time.

We managed a few salmon, but the fishing was slowing down. There were even a few giant dobsonflies around, but although trout and salmon usually love these things, they didn't seem interested. There was the thought that the fish were comatose in the warming water or actually absent, having already retreated to the deeper, cooler lakes to wait out the summer. That happens every year, but it's happening earlier with global warming, making fly-fishing even less dependable than it already is. This won't go down in the books as the worst effect of climate change, but to some of us it's not insignificant.

That night after dinner we sat on the porch of the lodge taking turns watching the bald eagles nesting on the far shore of Aziscohos Lake through binoculars while Rick told a story about his game warden days in New Hampshire. It seems that it's illegal in that state to keep landlocked salmon that are caught through the ice, but a fair number of fishermen were doing it anyway. So Rick trained a black Lab to sniff out these fish and played hell with the local poachers for a few years. To this day there are ice fishermen in the region who will dump their illicit salmon back down the hole at the mere sight of any black dog.

I suggested that tomorrow we take a boat out and troll streamers in the lake, which is a time-honored method in Maine. As a kid in Minnesota I considered trolling to be an antique form of punishment—like being forced to stand in the corner—made tolerable only because it might end in a walleye dinner, but later in life I've developed a taste for its monotony punctuated by unexpected moments of excitement. For one thing, you can do it with a fly rod. For another, you don't really have to stop talking to avoid scaring the fish. That was just something adults made up to keep the kids quiet. There were even some big trolling streamers for sale at the lodge, including a beautiful bucktail designed by Rick called a Bosebuck Little Trout, or BLT for short. But everyone begged off, saying they didn't have the right sinking lines. (Apparently it takes full lead-core lines to get the flies deep enough.) It was a warm, fragrant evening with the air filled with swallows, and we were all lazy from a big meal after a day of fishing. There was the strong sense of a trip winding down, as well as the inkling that I really should be at home, where I might not be of any help but where I could at least worry more effectively.

By the time I got back to Colorado the Waldo Canyon fire was under control and Ed and Jana were back home, although others in the area weren't so lucky. Ed used to be a firefighter with the Forest Service, and in his usual laconic way he said it was "interesting" to be on the other side of things for a change.

High Park was finally declared to be contained at precisely 87,284 acres, but it's understood that fires of this magnitude aren't really "out" until they're buried under snow, so there was still the possibility it could blow up again without warning. It was the thirtieth of June, with months of fire season left to go. My stuff was still piled inconveniently on the floor of my office ready to be grabbed and hustled to the car at a moment's notice, topped by that old picture of Dad looking like the Red Baron in his leather flight jacket and goggles. I decided to leave it all there until October.

6.

GETTING THERE

Traveling well is one of life's great pleasures, but the ability to stay coolly unflappable far from home is a moving target. For instance, a few years ago I was standing in a long, slow line at customs at the Montreal airport with my heart in my throat, and there was no reason for it. As far as I knew, my papers were in order; I wasn't carrying anything on the long list of prohibited items, and my shameful secrets were all too personal to turn up in a background check. Still, I was about to confront a uniformed officer in a foreign country, and the fact that I'd been let into Canada dozens of times over the last thirty-five years didn't seem to be a guarantee of success.

Finally I stepped up to the booth, where a tired-looking customs guy asked, "Purpose of your visit?"

"Fishing."

"Good luck," he said, handing me back my passport.

Up till then I'd felt like a beast of burden with my daypack, duffel, a long tube containing two spey rods, and an inexplicably guilty conscience, but just like that I was light on my feet again: an innocent man going about his business.

There was a minor speed bump when the LED readout on a pay phone insisted on giving directions in French, but then I found and pushed a little shiny button marked "English," and voilà! Likewise, the desk clerk at the hotel answered in *français*, but switched seamlessly to my mother tongue as soon as I started to speak. When I finally got to the hotel, I tipped the shuttle driver with some colorful Canadian bills that didn't seem like real money and said, *"Merci."* That's one of the handful of French words I know, but I hoped it made me sound passably cosmopolitan.

At that point I was still two and a half days and three flights from the coast of Labrador and had all but lost track of the idea of Atlantic salmon fishing, but I knew from experience that I'd regain it by degrees. Two mornings and two provinces later I'd board the first of two small planes with pontoons instead of wheels, and the rod tube would begin to seem less like an awkwardly shaped object I had to lug around and more like the key to the universe. In theory, that is, since Labrador is one of those places—like Alaska or the Northwest Territories—where arranging for a plane is more like placing a bet than actually booking a flight.

In the meantime, stopping for the night allowed me to relax from the hyperattentiveness of travel. After stashing my gear in my room, I went outside for a smoke and thought, *Okay, here I am, a man alone in a foreign city on his way to an adventure in the far north.*

Cities like Montreal are the final destination for many travelers, but fishermen rarely see much more than the airport and a hotel close enough to hear the jets coming and going before boarding the first in a series of shorter flights on progressively smaller airplanes. I hear stories of traveling anglers having fine meals and taking in the nightlife on stopovers, but my tendency is to eat within walking distance to save cab fare and then try to bank a good night's sleep against the tiredness that will inevitably arrive in the days to come.

The next night I checked into another hotel, this one in Labrador City, Labrador, a dreary iron-mining outpost that made no effort whatsoever to be rustic or charming. The centerpiece of the small lobby was a large painting depicting lumpish men standing in the snow amid unidentifiable machinery, while in the distance gray smoke belches into an equally gray sky. No scenic rivers or leaping fish.

This was an expensive hotel, not because it was anything special but because even shabby rooms are at a premium in this isolated settlement. The guests seemed to be about evenly split between fishermen in fleece vests and mining engineers in pressed khakis: one group excited about going into some of the last great wilderness in North America, the other just as giddy about turning the whole thing into a slag heap. The engineers were in the lobby working on laptops, while the fishermen were outside talking. I'd been down the street buying a tin of Watkins Bite Balm to soothe the blackfly welts I expected to get in the coming days and spotted this handful of guys in front of the hotel on my way back. They were taking turns holding their hands three feet apart, and I recognized them as members of my own tribe from a block away. One of these guys later told me that the previous year on the Hunt River he'd caught seventeen Atlantic salmon from a single pool in a single day. If he'd said seven, I might have believed him.

Across the street from the hotel was Peace Park, the town's only real attempt at civic improvement. It consisted of a brick sidewalk, a bush, and two benches in an otherwise open half acre of dandelions.

To the left of that was Jubber's Convenience store; to the right was a McDonald's and a Pizza Delight, and on the corner there was a billboard advertising "Cain's Quest: The most challenging snowmobile race on the planet" with a $100,000 purse. (Labrador is affectionately known to locals as "the land God gave to Cain.") Nothing here seems fabulously exotic, but so few Americans know where Labrador is (some think it's next to Norway) that it seems to exist outside the normal boundaries of geography.

These can be some of the great moments in fishing. I know it's supposed to be all about screaming reels, silver slabs, and drinks at the lodge—and it will be eventually—but sometimes just getting there is the largest part of the exploit. Mostly it's just the normal drudgery of travel: time, money, boredom, and the looming possibility of lost baggage and canceled flights, punctuated by odd uncomfortable moments, as when the scanner beeps and a security guy approaches with the electronic dildo they playfully refer to as a "wand."

But there's the possibility of real disaster, too. I once said that at a certain age, going down in a floatplane on your way to fish a remote river begins to look like one of the better ways to cash out, but however much you might mean that, it's still the kind of thing you say to friends over coffee as a way of sounding bravely levelheaded. If a plane really did auger in, I'd spend my last seconds like anyone else: bargaining with God and wetting my pants.

I end up pondering these things because some trips seem interminable and there's too much time to think, but at least I know I'm getting close to the fishing when I end up in a tiny airport like the one in Marquette, Michigan, where there were only two other people in the waiting room, one pecking at a computer, the other sleeping. When I said to the lady behind the ticket counter that it was "Kinda slow today," she said, "Oh sure, but, you know, by the time your plane comes there'll be fifteen or twenty people in here."

Or the one in Yellowknife in the Northwest Territories, where I was informed that my plane would leave an hour and a half late not because of weather or mechanical problems but because "Some guys flying in from Winnipeg are running late, so we're gonna wait for 'em."

It's less common for strangers to speak to each other in airports than it used to be—people are now mostly swiping at the screens of smartphones like monkeys intrigued by shiny objects—but it does still happen. A few kind souls recognize me from my books, but most just pick me out of the anonymous crowd as a fellow fisherman. In Portland, Oregon, a man tells me, without preamble, that he's going sturgeon fishing in the Columbia River, where he'll be using a salt-water spinning rod, shark hooks, and half a chicken as bait because the fish grow so big. Why should I, of all people, care? It's obvious to both of us.

In Minneapolis a man in a suit carrying a laptop nods at my rod case and says, "I'll trade you this computer for one of those fly rods." I say, "No thanks," and we grin at each other as if we'd just improvised the best gag ever.

In Seattle a man carrying a backpack and a rod tube asks me if I'm going fishing.

I say, "No, I'm on a book tour."

"Well, better luck next time," he says.

And an odd thing happened the last time I passed through Montreal. Always before, people had spotted me as an American from a block away—no telling how—but on the last trip strangers suddenly began addressing me in French. What was that about? Had repeated exposure to the north woods finally given me enough regional ease to seem French Canadian? Whatever; at a coffee kiosk in the airport I noticed that the barista was speaking French, so I took my best shot, ordered a *"Petit café, s'il vous plaît"* in what sounded, even to me, like a Colorado accent, and got a look that seemed to be equal parts incomprehension and disgust.

Cultural misunderstandings—large and small and usually harmless—

come with the territory. Once, years ago on a stopover in Inverness, Scotland, on the way to the River Beauly, a man told me, "We have a statue here of the greatest poet who ever lived."

"You have a statue of Allen Ginsberg?" I asked.

"No, lad; *Robert Burns!*"

Long drives are preferable to flying in many ways, but they can produce their own brand of misery. If you have company, there's usually a few hours of conversation that eventually sputters into a companionable silence and then the kind of boredom that's somehow more oppressive than if you were by yourself. But boredom is preferable to the seemingly endless games of "Name This Band" that two amateur rock historians I often travel with fall into, in which they go back and forth playing the first few bars of obscure deep cuts from thirty years' worth of rock and roll—roughly from Iron Butterfly to Nirvana—trying to stump each other.

I usually don't take part because they know this stuff better than I do, they're quicker, and, frankly, because in middle age I've begun to form a kind of immunity to music. It's not that I don't like it anymore; it's just that my fondest memories of music involve concerts and guitars on back porches, while now it's blared indiscriminately in public places with the intention of making shoppers more docile. You can't get away from it, and it's invariably the kind of corny top-forty schlock from the 1970s and '80s that made my teeth hurt even when it was new.

Anyway, this game eventually begins to rub me the wrong way, because just when I get into a tune and start to boogie a little, someone names the band and they turn it off and go on to another cut. The urge to scream wells up, and somewhere around the three-hundred-mile mark I begin to wonder why these guys are my friends and why we've traveled and fished together for so long. But to be fair, at *four* hundred miles even the Dalai Lama would start to get on my nerves.

But eventually the game, like the conversation, peters out, and there's nothing much to think about except the precise dosing of the coffee (enough to keep you wired, but not so much that you're peeing every half hour) and the timing of gas stops. In large parts of the American West, gas stations are few and far between, so I make it a practice to fill up at half a tank, just in case. That's a habit left over from when I drove a 1966 V8 Ford that got a whopping seven miles to the gallon. In the course of those years, I stopped at least once at every gas station in five western states. The good news was gas cost forty cents a gallon. The bad news was the minimum wage was two dollars an hour, and as a trout bum I worked for the minimum wage, when I worked at all.

But I do love driving around the Mountain West, even though the distances can be daunting. (Why is a question hardly worth asking. Sometimes it's as simple as that there are no steelhead in my time zone.) I got the bug as a kid growing up in the flat, domesticated Midwest watching John Wayne westerns, but not even Cinemascope could adequately convey the wide-open spaces. I remember my first live view of the Rocky Mountains through a windshield in the late 1960s. From a vantage point somewhere in eastern Colorado, I mistook the snow-capped peaks on the western horizon for an enormous storm front and began to brace for bad weather. When I realized my mistake, I had to pull over and get out of the car, not so much to enjoy the view as to come to terms with my disorientation.

The same kind of thing still happens forty-some years later. I've gotten used to the scale of things and do take it all for granted at times, but now and then I'll be pumping gas in ninety-degree heat while gazing at snowfields that don't seem all that far away, even though I now know they are. I'll think, *Between here and there are two rivers, a dozen tributaries, and hundreds if not thousands of trout. Holy shit!*

So you keep one eye on your destination—which can be days away—and the other on the fabulously empty and constantly changing landscape, reminding yourself that tourists make this trip for its own sake. Driving anywhere in the West is like traveling by hot-air balloon: it takes forever to get anywhere, but you can't beat the view.

Still, the monotony can be mind numbing, especially when you're alone. I usually drive the regulation five or six miles an hour over the limit that folklore says any cop will give you, but real speeding is no longer the temptation it once was. It's probably an early symptom of geezerhood that the speed limits I once assumed were made by and for old fogies now seem about right. For that matter, my fifteen-year-old pickup will go eighty or ninety in a pinch, but when it does it always reminds me of that scene in every episode of *Star Trek* when Scotty calls the bridge to say, "If I push her any harder, she'll shake apart!" I avoid using cruise control, because keeping my speed where I want it gives me something to do. So does grazing the radio dial, if only to see how many stations are simultaneously broadcasting Rush Limbaugh.

Music of my own choosing helps, but the radio is unreliable, and I don't carry a large supply of my own. (My most recent used pickup is new enough to have a CD player instead of a tape deck, but I've been slow to upgrade and have only a handful of CDs.) Bob Dylan almost always works, but something like "Visions of Johanna" can put me into a poetic spiral that makes me want to stop and sit staring at the clouds. And once, while listening to Willie Nelson, I had a disturbingly detailed vision of myself as an old man living alone in a trailer in eastern Wyoming, drinking instant coffee, reading used paperbacks from the Goodwill store, and feeding a dozen stray cats. There's nothing wrong with spending time in your own head, but it's best not to start turning over rocks to see what crawls out.

On the other hand, I sometimes fantasize about moving for a season to one of the river towns I pass through, where I'd patiently learn the water—mostly on my own, but also with occasional advice from friendly locals—and then write a book about it. This wouldn't be a fish-choked destination river, but a second- or third-class stream two or three states from home; someplace that is uncrowded, unremarkable at first glance, with a town where I could rent a trailer or maybe an unused summer cabin stuck in limbo between the death of the surviving parent and the eventual sale by the grown kids. I learned decades ago that if you're itinerant and persistent, you can usually sniff out a cheap, temporary place to live. Maybe I could even find free digs in return for caretaker and handyman chores and draining the pipes when I leave.

I'd go light, with just fishing tackle, clothes, a box of books, and a laptop. In the book I'd write I would cleverly leave the river unnamed and its location unspecified in order to make it seem mythological. I've given this a lot of thought, but I've been careful not to compose even a single sentence of the actual book, because that could ruin the fantasy. E. B. White said that a book is never so good as it is just before you start writing it.

I've never actually done this, and that might be for the best. When I confessed this pipe dream to an old friend he said he liked the idea, but added, "Knowing you, you'd probably just end up working in a gas station and dating a local widow."

I've found it's also best to avoid reliving old slights, wrongs, and grudges on long, solitary drives. These things are always in there somewhere, and they can be earworms that slip through the smallest cracks in your concentration and into the light of day. Without warning, and seemingly out of nowhere, you're livid all over again at the dickwad boss who fired you for no reason back in 1971, thinking of all the things you should have said and done but didn't, and filling your system with useless adrenaline. When this begins to happen, immediately loosen your grip on the wheel, take long, deep breaths, and go to your happy place while you still have one. It all happened over forty years ago, and the guy was old even then. Surely he's dead by now, while you're alive and well and going fishing.

Falling asleep is another constant hazard. You'll see the early symptoms of highway hypnosis in others whenever you pull into some roadside joint for a break. Everyone in the parking lot over the age of thirty-five is unfolding themselves stiffly, rubbing cobwebs off their faces, and blinking at their surroundings as if they'd just come out of comas, which in a way they have. I've never fallen asleep while driving, although I've learned to identify the telltale signs of dreaminess, like passing through small towns without noticing or imagining that the tumbleweeds blowing across the road in failing light are actually a flock of wild turkeys. But I've been a passenger in vehicles where the driver *did* fall asleep, and there's no more helpless feeling. This has happened three times in my life, and the odds seem slim that I'd survive a fourth.

And of course on any solitary drive lasting ten hours or more, I invariably fall deeply, though briefly, in love with at least one truck stop waitress. I remember a girl somewhere along Interstate 15: early thirties, long blond hair, black halter top, extremely short cutoff blue-jean skirt. She's wearing the bemused expression of someone who's used to being stared at by strange men just passing through, while the men themselves seem furtive and tight-lipped from the effort of holding in their potbellies. Maybe she hopes she has a future somewhere far from the Flying J Truck Stop in Idaho, with its perfume of grease and diesel fumes. For an instant you imagine she's just waiting for someone—possibly an older man with experience—to take her away from all this.

On the way back to the pickup it suddenly occurred to me that I'd left the reel with the 8-weight line on it at home, so I unlocked the topper and desperately pawed through my duffel bag looking for it. It was there, of course. No problem. I just got a little rattled for some reason.

7.

MY JEEP

At a family reunion, my ninety-two-year-old mother asked me what was new, and I told her, among other things, that I'd bought a Jeep. She said, "You've always wanted a Jeep, ever since you were a little boy." Then she added, in a less wistful tone of voice, "And anyway, you need it for your fishing." I took that as absolution. We native midwesterners are not the frivolous kind who would fork over hard-earned money for something just because we wanted it, but as a fisherman living in the Rocky Mountains, I *needed* a Jeep, the way a farmer needs a tractor—never mind that he's wanted a tractor ever since he was a little boy.

For years I made do with a succession of four-wheel-drive pickups that imperfectly split the difference between work, road trips, day-to-day errands, and the bad roads that led to good trout fishing. That accomplished the frugal goal of not having to buy, license, insure, and maintain more than one vehicle, but pickups have their limits, as I discovered years ago when I was still exploring the region I now call home. There was an obscure two-track that ran from the flats down to a creek in the next drainage that I wanted to check out. The road looked okay on the map (famous last words), and it was, except for one pitch that was steep, narrow, serpentine, washed out, boulder strewn, and canted precipitously sideways. It was the dry-land equivalent of class-five rapids, but by the time I realized I didn't want to try it, I was too far in to back out.

It didn't help that I was in the wrong vehicle: a full-sized three-quarter-ton pickup with a big V8 engine. This truck was the kind of indulgence some men of my generation allowed themselves back in the days of cheap gas and blissful ignorance about emissions. It had all the power and load capacity you could want, but in spots like this it was just too damned big and clumsy for its own good.

There was no alternative but to try to make it down that road. It felt like a slow-motion train wreck, although technically I was in full control of the vehicle the entire time. (Unbuckling my seat belt and propping the door open in case I had to bail out were just precautions.) At the bottom of the hill I checked the undercarriage to see if any of the hideous scrapes and bangs I'd heard on the way down had punctured my oil pan and was relieved to see that they hadn't. I was also glad there was another road out to the state highway. It was longer by more than a mile and plenty rough in its own right, but I'd been on it before and knew it wasn't life threatening. Later a friend informed me that only dirt bikers used that old road down from the flats. "And you did it in that big truck?" he said. "Jeez!"

I've gone through any number of four-wheel-drive pickups since then, most of them smaller and more agile, but they still had the common failings of a wheelbase that was too long and clearance that was too low for more advanced off-road maneuvers. And although it's not strictly true that the best high country trout fishing is always at the end of the gnarliest road, it's true often enough. I once drove a friend from back east to a sweet little trout stream at an elevation of around nine thousand feet. He liked the creek, with its mix of brook trout and cutthroats, but he was appalled at the washed-out old logging road that resembled a dried-up streambed. I'd told him we'd be going in on a dirt road. We hadn't gone far when he said, "Where I come from, a dirt road is, you know, *dirt*. This is all, like, *rocks* and shit!"

For several years a friend would lend me his Jeep Wrangler for the kind of roads that had contributed to the shortened lives of some of my previous pickups. I was never sure why he was so generous, except that he's a nice guy and a fisherman who's often too busy to go fishing himself but doesn't hold it against those of us who *can* go. I told him I'd be as careful as possible with his Jeep. He said he trusted me because I knew what I was doing when it came to off-road driving. (I didn't remind him that I'd once earned the nickname "Hard-on" for being so hard on equipment.) Beyond that, I followed the advice of a favorite uncle about borrowing cars: "Don't abuse the privilege," he said, "and always return it with a full tank."

So I was in fat city for a few seasons, but then my friend's fortunes changed enough that he could no longer justify the expense of a second vehicle—especially one that I used more than he did. He sold it for more than I wanted to pay, but by then I was irreparably spoiled, so I went shopping for a Jeep of my own.

By "Jeep" I don't mean the various cars and trucks that have borne that brand name over the years; I specifically mean the commercial version of the World War Two military quarter-ton 4x4 that first appeared on the market in 1945 as the CJ. (The initials stood for "Civilian Jeep.") That first Jeep was long on practicality and short on luxury: sprung hard, geared low, and with no frills. It was envisioned as a light agricultural vehicle—an early model, the CJ-2, was called the "Agrijeep"—but the vehicles quickly caught on with the general public, and later models became progressively more carlike. The newer Wranglers are fancier and more comfortable, but they still bear a striking family resemblance to the old, no-nonsense CJs: there are still drain plugs in the floor, and they're still small and compact, with the tight turning radius and short, eighty-inch wheelbase that lets you tiptoe over boulders that would high-center a pickup.

I thought finding a good used one would be easy, because Jeeps are ubiquitous here in northern Colorado as family cars, off-road vehicles, and fashion statements. It's hard to make the fifty-mile round-trip to Boulder without seeing a dozen of them, from shiny new Rubicons to venerable CJ-5s and anything in between.

But Jeepology is a room with a thousand doors. Behind one is the military collector who wants a fortune for anything that's painted olive-drab and has a crisp white star on the door, while behind the next is the guy with an elderly Jeep from the 1940s. It's parked out back in the weeds on flat, bald tires, its brake lines have been eaten by rabbits, its hoses and belts are rotted, and mice are living in the upholstery. But he's real proud of it because it was built by Willys Motors, the original Jeep manufacturer. "That's pronounced 'Willis,' not 'Willees,'" he says, as if correcting a third-grader.

Some Jeep owners have felt moved to pull the original four- or six-cylinder engines and replace them with overpowered V8s so they'll go really fast. As an afterthought, they've also had to cobble together beefed-up cooling systems because the little Jeep radiators couldn't handle the added strain. When you ask these folks why, they just look at you.

Others lean toward chrome stacks, rhino guards, light bars, painted flames, screaming-skull decals, dump truck–sized tires, and lifts so high you need a stepladder to get into the driver's seat. "Nice," you say politely, "but not quite what I'm looking for."

Among the used stock Jeeps I found were plenty whose owners had been doing with them what I intended to do, and so they'd been driven nearly to death. Some no longer ran but might with extensive repairs, while many that did run qualified as walking wounded. I took one I was interested in to a garage and asked a guy named Scott to look it over. Half an hour later he walked out of the shop, wiping his hands on an oily rag, and asked, "Are you a good shade-tree mechanic?"

"No, I'm not," I said.

"Well, then, don't buy this Jeep."

A salesman at a dealership was familiar with the problem. "You don't want a used Jeep that was driven by a hard-core four-wheeler," he said. "You want one that was owned by a sorority girl who drove it around town because she thought it was cute."

My friend Vince helped me shop for a Jeep, partly out of the genuine goodness of his heart and partly because if I found the right one at the right price, he'd get to go fishing in it. Vince knows more about Jeeps than I do, and he's a large man and former bodybuilder who can be usefully imposing when it comes to haggling. I'm not exactly a babe in the woods myself, but when the annoyingly slick dude at the car lot says, *I think you guys are being unreasonable*, Vince is the one who can deliver a line like, *You're a used-car salesman; no one cares what you think*, with the authority of a Detroit hit man.

In fact, it was Vince who found the Jeep I finally bought. He called me on his cell phone and said he was standing next to a 2000 Wrangler parked on the outskirts of a nearby town. He read me the particulars off the for-sale sign, including the six-figure mileage, and said, "I think you should drive out here and look at this."

I did, and two days later, after the usual tire kicking, test driving, and dickering, I bought it for a little more than I'd hoped to spend, but not too much more than I could afford. You know how it is: there was more to this than just simple transportation. Robert Downey Jr. once said, "Money can't buy you happiness, but it can buy you a yacht big enough to pull up right alongside it." Compared to even a small yacht, my new twelve-year-old Jeep was a steal. I pictured myself driving up alongside happiness and walking the rest of the way with a daypack and a fly rod.

The shakedown cruise was up a road I use as a personal benchmark, in the sense that I won't knowingly attempt anything worse. It runs for about three and a half miles, with two fords and several white-knuckle features, including one boulder pile that's widely known as the speed bump from hell—a short pitch of large rocks with deep washouts in between and a hard left turn just where it climbs steeply uphill. So many people have turned around here that there's an improvised wide spot in the road. Others who *should* have turned around but didn't have left the rocks scraped, skid-marked, and oil-stained.

This road finally dead-ends at a wilderness area boundary within sight of my favorite mountain creek: a sweet little thing that's as good as it is because the god-awful trail to it weeds out the riffraff. When we got there, I leaned against a fender to put on my wading boots, enjoying the way the sound of the current harmonized with the ticking of the cooling engine. Vince and I covered a mile or so of the stream that day and caught lots of chubby, handsome little brook trout that were already in spawning colors even though it was only mid-August. I tied on the same fly I always use there—a size-16 Hare's Ear Parachute—and left it on all day, which is sort of the whole point. If you get far enough up a bad enough road, you can find trout that don't see a lot of flies.

The Jeep had done just fine on the way in—my tendency to ride the clutch notwithstanding—and Vince had narrated the hairier parts of the drive with stupendously filthy porn-film dialogue. I asked myself if I was being more or less careful with my own Jeep than I'd been with the borrowed one, and wondered what the answer would say about the quality of my character.

On the way out we stopped to talk to a man who was walking his young Labrador retriever. He admired the Jeep, and I told him I'd just gotten it. "What have you done to it?" he asked, and seemed disappointed to hear that I'd just had a tune-up and oil change and bought five new tires. He proceeded to tell us what he'd done to his own Jeep: a two-inch lift, titanium wheels, beefed-up suspension, a twelve-thousand-pound winch, a bank of driving lights, and so on. There are countless accessories intended to enhance a Jeep's performance and appearance, although many of them just succeed in tarting it up, and most four-wheelers are more impressed by an unadorned Jeep covered with mud.

I didn't bother asking the guy why he was a mile up this road on foot when he had such a spiffy Jeep. He was out with his Lab, and any dog worthy of the name would rather walk than ride.

Back out on the highway at fifty miles an hour, the pebbles that had lodged in the aggressive tread of my new oversized tires began to pop loose and hit the wheel wells with loud cracks. For the first few miles it sounded like we were taking scattered small-arms fire.

Understand that I don't four-wheel for sport—I *fish* for sport and occasionally four-wheel in order to get to the places where I want to do that—but I have nothing against those who do. In fact, I don't mind seeing them at all. For one thing, people who are out four-wheeling for fun seldom stop to fish. For another, almost to a person they'll stop and help if you're in trouble. Some of the more serious rigs are virtually set up as wreckers, and helpfulness is a characteristic of the enterprise. Some guys see it as a solemn duty, while others just enjoy the challenge; and if nothing else, rescuing some poor nimrod who tried to make it through in a minivan makes for a good story. *There he was,* they'll say, *in his Bermuda shorts and flip-flops, wondering how it all went so wrong.*

Getting stuck or breaking down off-road is always a possibility, and it's no small thing. Friendly strangers don't always happen by, and even if they do, they can't always help. AAA won't come get you, and the recovery services that will can be hard to find and expensive, although chances are they'll be ready for anything, including those drivers who thought four-wheel drive would make them ten feet tall and bullet-proof. The level of assistance some of these outfits offer hints at the kind of epic trouble some people get into while four-wheeling: rollover towing, deepwater retrieval, burned vehicle removal.

The safe play is to avoid the worst calamities—even if that means parking the Jeep and walking the rest of the way—while being prepared to get yourself out of any lesser fix you might get into. With that in mind, I have a forty-eight-inch Hi-Lift jack and a tow strap (which, used together in conjunction with a chain and a handy tree, can double as a primitive and somewhat risky winch), plus a short D-handled shovel for digging out and backfilling and a bow saw for pruning the occasional deadfall. This is about the minimum equipment-wise, plus a bumper mount for the jack and bungees to secure the shovel and saw to the roll bar so they don't bounce around and smash your fly rod.

Remember the fly rod? After all, the whole idea here was just to go fishing.

8.

ALASKA

It was six a.m. when Doug and I boarded one of a pair of water taxis—along with all the other fishermen and half the guides from the lodge—for the hour-long run down to Dillingham to catch an early plane to Anchorage. Our flight from Anchorage to Denver was a red-eye that didn't leave until almost midnight, and we were idly wondering what we'd do with the twelve-hour layover. Killing that much time in a city usually runs into more money than you care to spend, while killing the same amount of time stuck at the airport can result in fatal boredom. (There *is* a mount of an albino beaver at the Anchorage terminal that's worth seeing, but it's not what you'd call endlessly entertaining.)

But of course, we'd gotten ahead of ourselves. By the time we got there, Dillingham was socked in with pea-soup fog, and our flight was first delayed and then canceled. It was more complicated than it should have been to get ourselves booked on an afternoon flight, but not as complicated as it was for the guy in front of us, a surgeon who'd been at the lodge with us. He had to rebook his entire trip so he could make it to a city on the East Coast by about the same time the following morning. Why? Because he had six operations scheduled for that day. I wondered if there was a way to warn this guy's patients that he'd be cutting them open after going for twenty-four hours without sleep, but I couldn't think of anything.

Then we went looking for a cup of coffee but couldn't find any. "What the hell kind of airport doesn't have coffee?" Doug asked rhetorically.

Eventually some of us took the lodge van into greater downtown Dillingham—all three blocks of it—and had lunch across the road from the docks at a place called the Muddy Rudder, which is a common nautical euphemism. A commercial fisherman who runs his boat aground will say he got his rudder a little muddy in the same way that a bush pilot who crashes a plane and lives will admit that he may have "dinged up the aircraft."

Back at the fogbound airport we learned that our new flight was also delayed indefinitely. We came to understand that this was a different flight number but the same airplane. It had been diverted that morning from Dillingham to King Salmon, where it had been sitting all this time grounded by the weather. Among its passengers was the next batch of clients for the lodge, and I spared a kind thought for those other stranded fishermen. Some would be pissed off at the delay, while others would be at peace with the knowledge that the largest part of the adventure in Alaska is often just getting where you're going; but either way they'd have anticipation to keep them going.

There's nothing like that on the return leg. Coming home after a trip is one of life's simple pleasures, but a stack of unpaid bills and a full answering machine don't hold a candle to de Havilland Beaver floatplanes and salmon. Even the stories you hear in Alaska have the peculiar flavor of the place and could not have just as easily happened in Pittsburgh.

For instance, at a fly-in camp where we spent some time there was a walrus skull in the usual pile of collected antlers and bones that accumulates around a spike camp. I'd never seen a walrus skull before, but there was nothing else it could have been. It was missing the valuable tusks (they'd been traded to a native ivory carver), but the shape of what was left was unmistakable.

The story was that this enormous dead animal had washed in from the Bering Sea on a high tide and settled within sight of camp. Apparently a decomposing walrus smells about like you'd expect, and within twenty-four hours it had attracted a dozen brown bears. A walrus can weigh well over a ton, so for much of that season bears could be seen and heard at all hours feeding on and fighting over the carcass, and were sometimes found wandering through camp belching and farting and looking for a comfortable place for a nap.

Business went on as usual, and somehow there were no serious incidents, but late one night a fisherman woke up with an urge to relieve himself, stepped out of the tent—still half-asleep—and came face-to-face with a large bear reeking of putrid walrus blubber. The way the man told it, he quietly stepped back inside the tent, pissed in the corner, and went back to bed. Did he sleep? I don't know; that wasn't part of the story. Would you have slept?

I have many firsthand memories from the time we spent at that camp, but one of the most vivid is of something I can only imagine: namely, the expression on that guy's face when he bumped into that bear. For some reason, I imagine him looking as tight-lipped and vacant as George Washington on a one-dollar bill.

This is the kind of thing guides, outfitters, and lodge managers regularly deal with in Alaska. The backcountry is actually a fairly benign place as long as you either know what you're doing or are with someone who does, but bush planes, small boats, and large wild animals still pose inherent dangers that are complicated by the remoteness of a region where emergency-response times are measured in days rather than minutes. The list of things that can go south is so long that it's amazing trips go as smoothly as they usually do, but the potential for serious trouble is always there.

Some adopt a cavalier attitude and begin to cut corners and take chances, while others get as careful and deliberate as little old ladies, but it doesn't seem to matter. If you spend enough time at this, the odds are good that you'll either live through a real horror show or at least get a couple of bad scares. Most of the folks at these lodges love what they're doing, and it shows. Furthermore, they understand that they're essentially in the hospitality business, so, with the odd grumpy exception, they tend to be pretty hospitable. But in quiet moments you can still catch glimpses of the thousand-yard stare. It's a look that says, without rancor, *You're here for a week; I've been here for ten years.*

My own tendency is to prepare for the mishaps that are foreseeable and otherwise hope for the best, but I can understand the come-what-may attitude you sometimes see, because so many of the things that go sideways in Alaska fall outside the purview of anyone's backup plan.

I once heard an awful first-person survival story. A party of four bear hunters was flown into a remote location and dropped off. They were in a small plane, and the outfitter said he could take only them but that he'd return in a few hours with all their gear and provisions and the guide. The man who was telling the story said that since they'd be left in bear country, he insisted on bringing a rifle and a box of shells, but that was it. It was fall. They were dressed in street clothes, tennis shoes, and light jackets. The plane dropped them off and never came back. They would learn much later that the so-called outfitter had set them up. There was no bear hunt and no guide. The guy had taken their money, gear, rifles, and the plane and vanished, leaving them to die.

They waited for several days with a gathering sense of panic and then started walking roughly in the direction they'd come, skirting bogs, climbing hills, and trying to go in as much of a straight line as the terrain would allow. They walked for weeks. *Weeks!* They were wet, cold, and exhausted, and although they had a rifle, they saw no game, so they were also starving. They assumed they'd die—the only question was when and in what order—and finally one of the four sat down and refused to go on. The narrator said he slapped the man in the face as hard as he could and said, "We'll rest for ten minutes, and then we're leaving. You can either stay or come along; it's up to you." Ten minutes later the man struggled to his feet and came along.

Eventually they came to a lake where fishing boats were passing a few hundred yards out, presumably heading back to port, given the time of day. They yelled and waved and fired the rifle in the air trying to attract attention, but the fishermen assumed they were drunken locals whooping it up and ignored them. Finally, in desperation and with only two shells left, one of them put a round into the hull of a passing boat. A few hours later a boatload of police officers arrived to arrest them and they were rescued.

These four men had all been friends, but the one who almost gave up and was saved by that slap in the face never spoke to the others again.

I've run into quite a few guys who have retired from decades of guiding or outfitting in Alaska. (None of them was rolling in money, which is something to think about if this kind of life appeals to you as a career opportunity.) I can't exactly spot them from a distance, but they do all have the grizzled look of lifelong outdoorsmen on Social Security, and they're typically full of stories that they're not shy about telling. Some are about big fish, but most involve the plane crashes, boat wrecks, maulings, heart attacks, disappearances, and dozens of other close calls that are bound to happen over time and that wear on your nerves. These guys sometimes beat around the bush when it comes to why they finally pulled the plug on Alaska and moved back to civilization. "It's a young man's game" they'll say, or "Your heart has to be in it," although a few come right out with "I just got too old for that shit."

One day at that fly-out camp with the walrus skull we motored far up a small coastal river to where the guides said there'd be large Dolly Vardens and maybe some big rainbows following the spawning chum salmon. Part of me wanted to stay in the lower river and fish for king salmon as we'd done successfully the day before, but the guides, Tyler and Matt, whom I knew from a previous trip, really wanted to go upriver. "You'll love it," they said, adding that they hadn't fished up there all season, and if they hadn't, no one had.

Doug and I talked it over and thought, *Why not?* When guides want to do something outside the normal program, it can be fabulous or a wild goose chase, but it's always interesting.

It was a long, harrowingly fast run upriver in the jet boat. Doug and I sat side by side on the middle bench. Matt was ahead of us with his hood up and his head down against the drizzling rain. Tyler stood in the stern running the motor and listening to Pink Floyd through earphones, which he said helped his concentration.

Where we stopped the river had shrunk to the size of a respectable creek, flowing through thick alders and willows that grew right down to the banks. Tyler had mentioned offhandedly that there "might be some bears up there." That didn't register back at camp, because it's true anywhere you go in this region, but when I saw how tight the cover was, I realized that any bear you saw here was likely to be at desperately close range. I mentioned that to Matt, and he allowed that they did "loom up unexpectedly" from time to time.

74

Doug and I strung up our rods and began to fish downstream. Before they began following along behind us walking the boat, Matt slipped a short-barreled .44 Magnum revolver into a shoulder holster and Tyler chambered a round in a 12-gauge pump and laid it conveniently on the bow. That was comforting, even though the presence of firearms isn't a guarantee of safety. In fact, guns can have the opposite effect by causing you to swagger confidently into places you shouldn't go.

No need to pointlessly build drama here. We never saw a bear, although they were as thick as raccoons and had left multiple fresh tracks and impressive turds on every available sandbar. Some of the scat was glisteningly fresh and steaming and couldn't have been more than a few minutes old. One set of tracks was made by two cubs and a large sow, whose maternal instinct would make her the most dangerous animal in North America.

We caught plenty of Dollys and a handful of rainbows. My snapshots reveal that many were large but not record-breaking, and I have to rely on my memory of how pretty they were. It was a wet day with uncertain light, and I don't know how to operate a camera beyond which button to push to take the picture, so they came out as either black silhouettes or translucent silver, like ghost fish.

I felt that I'd fished brilliantly that day, owing to hyperalertness and the creepy sense that something large, carnivorous, and unsympathetic was breathing down my neck. On the other hand, I have to admit that dragging orange plastic beads through pods of wild fish gorging on salmon eggs isn't the most challenging thing you can do with a fly rod. Still, there was the uncomplicated purity of doing a simple thing in a place as old as the world where no one else had fished that year. For those few hours there was no past or future, just an undeniably vivid *now*.

When we finally boarded our plane in Dillingham, six hours late, that's what I thought about on the way to Anchorage.

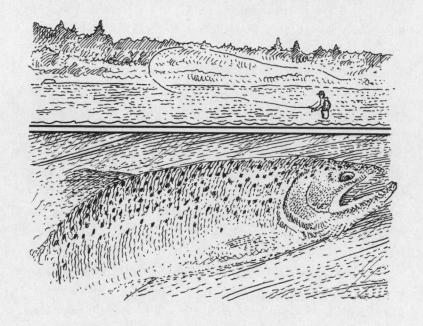

9.

THE VELVET HANDSHAKE

When we moved into the unoccupied fixer-upper some friends had
let us use, Vince immediately spread out his sleeping bag in the living room so I could bed down as far away from him as possible at the
back of the house. This kind of arrangement has become standard
procedure when we travel together. Vince snores ferociously, can't
help it, and feels guilty about it. On other trips I've seen him hand
out earplugs to unsuspecting victims, apologizing in advance.

This place had the musty abandoned-building smell that comes with disuse, but it freshened up quickly as we came and went, letting in cool outside air with each trip. We had electricity and running water, with a bucket under the kitchen sink in lieu of a drain. The furnace didn't work, but October wasn't that cold in this part of Washington State, and we could cut the morning chill by turning on the oven and leaving the door open while we brewed coffee and cooked breakfast.

We kept hearing what sounded like rifle shots muffled by distance. At first we thought it might be hunters in the nearby hills, but then we heard it only inside the house, never outside, and it kept up overnight. When we finally got curious enough to investigate, it turned out to be acorns falling on the roof from an overhanging oak tree.

We were spending our days road-fishing for steelhead and our evenings freeloading dinner at a small lodge farther up the valley. It was nothing fancy—just a refurbished ranch house with a few cabins out back and a garage made over into guides' quarters. Our friend Jeff was managing the place, and he said we should come up for dinner any night. I'm not sure any night meant *every* night, but that's how we took it.

When we asked the guides about the fishing, they said it had been slow, which is the kind of report you hear so often on steelhead waters that it no longer seems like news. Three years before, when we'd first fished here at the same time of year, conditions had been closer to ideal and the river was full of fish, but this season the fall rains were overdue and the region was stuck in a drought that had kept large wildfires burning for months, turning the setting sun into a sooty orange ball. The river was low, the sun was bright, and although some steelhead were in, the bulk of the run was still staged below the mouth of the river waiting for cloudy skies and a flush of water. Or at least, that was the guides' best guess. They were getting their clients into the occasional fish by dredging beads in the deepest holes, they said, but swinging flies had been "unproductive": a word that had the ring of finality.

We could have postponed the trip. In fact, we talked about it, but I had another trip later in the month that I didn't want to cancel, Vince had plans after that, then I had something else, and pretty soon it would be Christmas and we wouldn't have gone steelheading. When the river you have your eye on is a thousand-mile drive from home, the fishing takes on daunting proportions anyway, and if you then start weighing time and expense against weather and stream flow, you can end up dithering yourself right out of a fishing trip. But in the end we decided the best time to go fishing is when you can, so we did.

You never entirely come to terms with the dead spells in steelheading, but you do come to appreciate them as a kind of moral imperative, or as Marilyn Monroe supposedly said, "If you can't handle me at my worst, then you sure as hell don't deserve me at my best." In fact, you quickly get it through your head that fly-casting for any sea-run fish is a slow game that can still reward persistence. So when swinging flies is unproductive, the accepted solution is to keep swinging flies, fishing out every cast as if this were the *one*, because it could be. The first time I went steelhead fishing the river was also too low, the sun was too bright, and the fish were said to be either sulking or still milling around in Puget Sound. I fished for days without a pull and then landed my first two steelhead ever within fifteen minutes of each other. And on the evening of the last day, one of my partners, who'd been skunked up till then, got a big, bright fish literally on his last cast. We told him it was time to leave. He said, "Okay, let me just fish out this swing."

Vince and I started by going back to the pools where we'd hooked and either landed or lost fish the last time—a strategy that's as naïve as it is irresistible. We didn't have any trouble finding the spots. You might not remember all the places where you missed a trout three years earlier, but a lost steelhead is like a phantom limb: you know it's gone forever, but you'll never forget where it was.

We'd fall into the usual metronomic cast, swing, and step routine, covering water from the riffle at the head of a run all the way to the tailout. This feels like the kind of thing you'd do to kill time while waiting for inspiration—and sometimes it is—but in fact I've caught almost all my salmon and steelhead in this methodical way: shuffling and swinging along for hours at a time, waiting for the velvet handshake.

This is the kind of steady work that quiets the mind, as Wendell Berry said, so it would be dusk before we knew it. We'd walk back to the pickup, stow the rods, and drive up valley toward the lodge, wondering aloud what Jeff's wife, Jan, was cooking for dinner that night. She's one of those women who believe that food equals love, and as such, it doesn't have to be fancy but it should be really good, and there should be lots of it.

It would be full dark by the time we got there and joined the usual day's-end drill. Pickups towing drift boats pulled up in showers of dust and people clomped up onto the porch to hang rods in the rod racks, greet the camp dogs, exchange fishing reports, and peel off wet waders. There was the general upbeat energy of a shift ending. As much as you might love to fish, there's still that feeling of tired relief when you're finally off the water.

Inside it was like happy hour at a sports bar, with the same first-drink-of-the-night boisterousness as well as the perpetual football game turned up too loud on a sixty-inch TV sucking the oxygen from the room. And later, after a few more drinks, you'd overhear the same snatches of mismatched conversation in which one guy declares, "I think Glenn Beck is a genius," and someone else replies, "You mean *Jeff* Beck, right? The guitar player?" We realized that we had the rare opportunity here to cherry-pick the best of lodge life and deftly sidestep the rest. So after sponging a good meal we didn't have to cook for ourselves and picking the brains of the guides about where to fish the next day, we'd yawn theatrically, say it had been a long day, and head back to our quiet, empty house down the valley.

Steelhead—along with Atlantic salmon, the five species of Pacific salmon, and sea trout—all fit the unlikely profile of ocean fish that are born in freshwater rivers and return there to spawn, or river fish that spend much of their lives at sea, depending on how you look at it. It's an elaborate and risky adaptation (a hundred smolts can leave the river for every adult that survives to spawn), but it makes sense as an evolutionary blueprint. There's a lot more food in the ocean than in the river, so the fish grow bigger, and the biggest fish can claim the best spawning habitat and lay more eggs, thus ensuring the survival of the species. In this unforgiving system, reproduction is the only criterion for success.

Sea-run fish don't actively feed when they return to the rivers to spawn. The result is that they don't gobble up the parr from previous runs and decimate their own species, but no one seems willing to say that's *why* they don't eat. I once asked a why question in a college biology class. The professor said, "Here we talk about 'how'; if you want to know 'why,' you'll have to go over to the philosophy department." He pointed vaguely in the direction of the humanities building to show that he wasn't kidding.

I hate being hungry, so this idea of months of hardship without food haunts me. But then salmon are said to undergo physiological changes that may keep them from wanting to feed, which makes me feel better. Also, stomach-sample studies suggest that at least some steelhead secretly snack on the odd stonefly nymph or caddis pupa, and the whole business of fishing orange plastic beads for steelhead presupposes that they'll eat Chinook salmon eggs. That makes me feel a little better, too.

Some of these migrations are epic. Steelhead that entered salt water on the west coast have turned up over two thousand miles away in the Sea of Japan, where they fatten up on a rich diet of squid and forage fish before making the return trip to spawn. Once they're close, steelhead are said to locate their home rivers by smell, but scientists think these fish navigate the open oceans using the magnetite deposits in their nasal cavities. No one seems to understand how they do it, but why else would you have a magnet in your nose?

The system would look flawless on paper except that genetic diversity is maintained by the occasional fish that swims up the wrong river to spawn with strangers. My old biology professor wouldn't have been willing to say whether this was part of a master plan or just a happy accident that short-circuits the effects of too much inbreeding, while over at the humanities building they might have said, *Well, sometimes mistakes aren't really mistakes after all.*

The farthest inland I ever caught a steelhead was in the Salmon River in Idaho, some nine hundred river miles from the ocean. It was a big wild hen with old net scars and a half-healed seal bite. Before I landed her she got me in fast water and almost cleaned my clock, even though she might have traveled three thousand miles and hadn't eaten in the five or six months since she'd entered freshwater. Fishermen claim to love the sea-run fish for their size, but what we really love is the unimaginable size of their lives.

The elusiveness of these fish makes each one seem fraught with significance, and a cult of seriousness has grown out of the number of hours, days, or weeks that can pass between hookups. There's plenty that can go wrong without making a dumb mistake, so fresh leaders are bought before every trip, knots are tied with exaggerated care and lubricated with ChapStick before they're tightened, hooks are sharpened to surgical specifications, and favorite flies take on religious significance. It's widely believed that over time steadiness and diligence are rewarded, but it's also known that luck in steelheading is unevenly and unfairly distributed so that creeps and blowhards often land more than their share.

There are lots of crackpot theories about when, how, why, and what sea-run fish will bite when, by all rights, they shouldn't bite at all, but over the long haul none is so reliably productive as the one that says you should just keep a hook in the water. And although the tackle, tactics, and sometimes even the odd fly pattern will translate among species, the subcultures that have grown up around the various fish have stayed unique.

There are places, such as Maine, where there's a strong blue-collar tradition, but most still think of Atlantic salmon fishing as the Sport of Kings and associate it with private clubs, enforced gentility, fine tackle, single-malt scotch, and good cigars. There's a story that the cylindrical deer-hair Bomber fly was invented on the Miramichi River in New Brunswick when a wealthy sport tossed a cigar butt into the river and a salmon ate it. You assume it was an imported La Gloria Cubana instead of a rum-soaked crook bought at a gas station.

All things being equal, a good Atlantic salmon fisherman will do well on a steelhead river because the ground rules are so similar, but steelhead fishermen have a more rough-and-tumble reputation, and the salmon angler may find himself wondering if these people are entirely housebroken. Good scotch and cigars aren't unheard of in steelhead camps, but it's just as likely that instead of passing out Cubans, a steelheader will toss a Ziploc bag full of marijuana into the guides' shack the way you'd throw raw meat to a cage full of hyenas.

I've spent the last decade or so lagging behind the advancing technology of steelheading, not so much to be a Luddite as to strategically ignore the hot new thing until it either runs its course as an expensive fad or proves itself and becomes standard practice. I learned to cast two-handed rods with full floating lines and tapered leaders, and that's still my favorite way to do it, but there are too many times when you have to reach right down to the gravel to find fish. For that, most now use an assortment of Skagit heads and interchangeable tips of different lengths and sink rates that can be fine-tuned on the spot to achieve something approaching perfection. I was leery of these shooting heads for a while, then cautiously tumbled for them when they refused to go away. At first they felt as heavy and sluggish as lengths of wet rope, but in time my casts became crisper and more compact, my running line began to snake through the guides with a satisfying hiss, and my flies dove to the bottom like depth charges. Welcome to steelheading in the twenty-first century.

There's now a mind-numbing array of this stuff available commercially, but some spey-rod wonks aren't satisfied with any of it and spend hours in their basements with grain scales, scraps of line, razor blades, shrink tape, and heat guns building their own heads. You can spot these guys on the river by the way they scowl appraisingly at every cast, while back at the lodge their conversations run to lengths, grain weights, loop construction, and the arcane business of "cheaters." Steelheaders spend an inordinate amount of time and effort perfecting their casts because that's the only part of this process they have any control over. I catch myself admiring their restless dedication even as I try to reduce my own level of fussing to something more minimal.

We'd been told that the word had spread about this river since the last time we fished it, and there was some evidence of that. It wasn't exactly mobbed, but there were more cars on the canyon road, more fishermen in the general store every morning stocking up on coffee and breakfast burritos, and more drift boats on the river. Some, including those rowed by the guides from the lodge, would pass us on the inside in order to leave the runs undisturbed, while others would just pound beads and bobbers through our water, acting as though they hadn't seen us. Anadromous fish engender an insane devotion and, often enough to mention, the kind of self-importance that trumps manners. Maybe it's just human nature, or maybe it's zoology: a case of too many mammals competing for a limited and dwindling resource.

Once, on a famous steelhead river in Oregon, some friends and I launched a drift boat in the wee hours, hoping to be the first at an especially promising run. We made it, and for the next hour boats passed in the near dark and locals made rude comments about us and our mothers, maybe not realizing how well voices carry across water. But I'll take snubs and insults over the two guides in Alaska who recently beat each other senseless over a pod of king salmon while their sports stood by helplessly, wondering if this was part of the incomparable wilderness adventure they'd been promised.

One night after dinner, the owner of the lodge, Jack, found us out back with the guides and dogs and asked if we wanted to do a float through the canyon the next day. Were there fish up there? No telling, but we'd been pounding the lower river for days on the assumption that whatever steelhead were in would be stalled there waiting for the spate. We'd seen lots of other fishermen with the same idea, but no fish.

So in the morning we launched from a vacant campground just before dawn. We were high enough up the valley to be out of the scrub oak and into coniferous woods so deep green as to look black. There was fog on the water and a premonition of morning amber in the sky that was reminiscent of a Bob White painting, but no sign of steelhead. We swung limpid, fishy-looking pools and obscure tubs and rips that Jack pointed out. We tried different depths and different flies. A few other boats passed, and the fishermen in them shrugged in reply to the obvious question. We shrugged back. It's the international language of fishing.

That evening we ended up at a long, complicated run that was wide and bumpy with submerged boulders, slicks, and braided currents. Two spey casters from the lodge had already fished through it and were now far downstream, working their way into the tailout, while their guide relaxed in the boat, allowing himself a beer because this was the last run of the day, with the takeout right around the next bend. Vince and I spread out and started working down. I misread the current and my first swing was too fast, with the fly chasing the line almost straight across the river, so on the next cast I stripped off more line, threw more steeply downstream, and added a little mend. That felt better: a slow, deep, steady pull.

We were at that point in a blank trip where you can begin to lose the thread—and, in a way that's hard to explain, losing the thread can make a temporary slump permanent—but I remember feeling really good about this. For one thing, I liked this big, confusing run that probably didn't hide dozens of steelhead but could have, and after getting an angle on it I felt that on this pass, or maybe the next, I'd begin to understand how it was put together. For another, it was the time of day when things happen, with the sun off the river and the air turning chilly. Back home on my desk was a detailed list of things that would all take too much time and cost too much money but had to be done anyway, and I was happy to be on a distant river ignoring my life.

A fish hit hard on the inside of the main current and was into the backing before I fully grasped the idea that I'd hooked a steelhead. By then it was halfway down the run, where I could see Vince reeling in and backing out of the river to avoid fouling my line. This felt like a heavy fish (they all feel heavy at first), but with any luck, time would tell.

Jack waded in a little way downstream and stood leaning on his long-handled net; the guide in the boat downstream swiveled in his seat to watch the show, and I settled into the precarious sense of well-being that you don't have to describe to another steelheader and *can't* describe to anyone else.

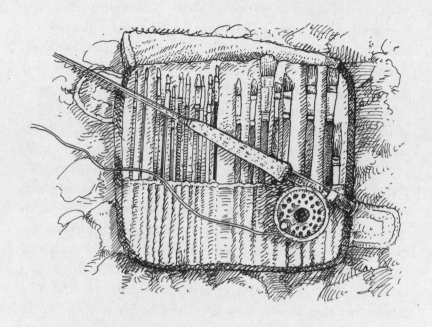

10.

GETTING IT RIGHT

I went fishing a few days after my mother died and not long before her funeral. This was after I asked my sister if she needed me for anything, and she said no, everything was being taken care of. The subtext here is that I'm not the one in the family anyone would trust with such important arrangements. Not a dark secret; just a fact.

I thought about canceling the trip anyway out of some antique sense of a proper period of mourning, but I could almost hear Mom asking, *Now what would be the point of that?* She was always relentlessly practical in the way of those midwestern women who grew up during the Great Depression, and she always gave me the benefit of the doubt about my seemingly aimless little adventures. During the years when Dad all but wrote me off as a hopeless wing nut, Mom agreed but thought it was okay because I was "creative." Or at least she hoped I was, because I was fairly useless by any other standard. They say you can't fool your mother and they're probably right, but they never said anything about your mother fooling herself.

So I packed my fishing gear, picked up my artist friend C.D. Clarke at Denver International Airport, and drove toward the North Park region of Colorado, up near the Wyoming border. When C.D. asked me what was new, I didn't mention the upcoming funeral, for the same reason some people who are managing chronic conditions like diabetes keep it a secret—that is, so as not to be needlessly treated like invalids. This may be a family trait. Mom had crippling arthritis for decades, but most days when you asked how she felt she'd say, "Fine," meaning, "Actually, I feel like hell, but I don't want to talk about it."

We gassed up on the outskirts of Fort Collins, then drove through Laporte and turned west up the Cache la Poudre River at Ted's Place, once a friendly little country store and café dating to the 1940s, now a gas station and convenience store where the clerk rings up your purchases from behind bulletproof glass. It was seventy-some slow, winding miles up the canyon, most of it within sight of the river, and C. D. naturally asked about it. I said I'd always felt it wasn't as good as it looked and that although I'd never actually been skunked there, I'd never done all that well, either. On the other hand, locals had told me that I just hadn't put in enough time to learn the river's peculiarities. An old story. Our dirt-road turnoff was right at Joe Wright Reservoir, with its unusual mix of grayling and rainbows, and we pulled into Rawah Ranch in midafternoon.

C.D. is a well-known "sporting artist," a term I'd avoid if I could think of something better, because in the larger art world it's sometimes meant condescendingly, as if an otherwise respectable painting becomes hopelessly corny the minute you put a fisherman in it. Better to say he's a fine artist who happens to deal predominantly in sporting subjects because they interest him, and so they now form a large part of his livelihood. He'd been invited here to paint and fish by the proprietor, Pat Timmons, and was told he could bring along a friend.

No one past the age of thirteen actually believes that a sporting artist lives a life of privileged luxury, traveling the world at will, hunting and fishing at places with gillies, chefs, and wine cellars, and, almost as an afterthought, dashing off a painting every once in a while, which then immediately sells for, like, a bazillion dollars. On the other hand, judging from questions I've heard people at fishing lodges ask, some are curious how close a working artist can come to that adolescent ideal.

C.D. is forthcoming enough that he may have some stock answers prepared. Yes, he does regularly travel the world: Canada, Alaska, England, Scotland, Iceland, the Caribbean, the Bahamas, and so on, where he does sometimes stay at pretty ritzy places, although not always, by a long shot. (The first time we fished together, we ended up in a tent in the rain.) Yes, he studied painting formally, and yes, he does make a living by selling his work.

But that's not what people are getting at. What they really want to know is, how do you *do* this? Is it hard work, or the kind of innate talent that appears effortlessly? Or do you just breathe different air than the rest of us? For that matter, do you live anything like a normal life, or do you spend your off hours sipping absinthe at sidewalk cafés with poets and philosophers? (Everyone's default vision of The Artist is set in 1920s Paris.) A few also wonder—but don't come right out and ask—is this just a way to get for free what the rest of us pay for? Or, as a kid in a fourth-grade class once asked me, "How much money do you make?"

How someone becomes successful in the arts when so many try

and fail is a fair question, but after making an uneven living as a writer for the last forty years, I understand that no two careers are alike, and that an honest and complete answer would be longer and more mundane than anyone really wants to sit through. Eventually you learn to politely answer direct questions without addressing the preconceptions behind them—leaving people vaguely disappointed—and also that it's best to let folks think whatever they want, including those who suspect you of running a scam.

As for that adolescent fantasy, C.D. told me that he *does* now and then accompany wealthy sports to places so exclusive most of us don't even know they exist to record the trip in oils and watercolors—sort of like a seventeenth-century version of a wedding photographer. I also know that on at least some of these expeditions he arranges to put away his brushes now and then to wet a line in some of the finest fisheries on the planet.

He's not an employee on these trips, and the clients don't own the paintings, but they do get first dibs on them, either the small ones he does on-site or larger versions of the originals that he produces later in the studio. It's also possible for a client to have himself painted into a composition if he's not there already.

Roughly along those same lines, C.D. once did a slyly goofy cover painting for *Fly-fishin' Fool* by James Babb. It's a standard scene of a man fly-casting on a placid, forested river, except that the fisherman is wearing a medieval-style tricornered fool's cap. According to a reliable source, when someone said they'd buy the painting if it weren't for that stupid hat, C.D. painted it out.

When he's staying at a lodge, C.D. will usually prop his finished paintings in the common room, where people can look at them at their leisure. This is a courtesy to those who are curious but too shy to snoop or come right out and ask to see the work—although if someone wants to know if a certain painting is for sale, well, there's a good chance it is.

People do wonder about the business end (the first question the parents of an aspiring artist ask is, "But how will you make a living?"), and the artist as working stiff isn't the first thing that comes to mind. What does come to mind might be Gauguin painting naked ladies in the South Seas; or van Gogh, the misunderstood genius who sold only one painting in his lifetime; or maybe Salvador Dalí, the playful surrealist who famously said, "The only difference between me and a madman is that I'm not mad."

In fact, everyone comes at it differently. Some depend on galleries, while others operate their own websites and save the commissions, and a successful artist I know trusts his wife to handle all the business. "If it weren't for her," he said, "I'd still be hawking paintings on street corners," which of course is another way to do it. Few artists think of their work as merchandise, but they're all glad *someone* does, and there are angles to everything that you wouldn't have thought of. I once asked a children's author how he went about writing for little kids. He said, "I *don't* write for little kids; I write for their mothers, because they're the ones who buy the books." As for C.D., he's as plainspoken as his paintings: happy enough to answer questions, but just as content to let people study the paintings while he stands at a polite distance—robust, dark haired, and, as a mutual friend pointed out, bearing a striking resemblance to Clark Kent. All that's missing are the horn-rimmed glasses.

For the next few days we fished the two miles of the Big Laramie River that the lodge owns. The river rises in the Medicine Bow Mountains in Colorado before it flows north into Wyoming, and this high in the drainage it's a medium-sized creek running in leisurely meanders down a mountain valley. It's a typical meadow stream, with riffles, deep pools, undercut banks, and the usual snags, brush piles, and sweepers that accumulate in water like this. There would have been a natural temptation to manicure the stream to cut down on casting and fish-playing obstacles for paying customers, but here they've left things as they are, maintaining it as the good trout water it is, and incidentally giving the fish the tactical advantage.

The valley is half a mile wide with slopes forested in lodgepole pine, fir, and aspen and a floor covered in dense, nearly impenetrable willows. The rustling of leaves in a breeze sounds so much like running water that you sometimes can't tell one from the other, and the overall effect is of a continuous sigh. There are moose signs everywhere, and now and then an actual moose, looking big, dark, and imperturbable. The Shiras moose that live in Colorado are the smallest of the four subspecies in North America, but when you bump into one in a willow thicket armed only with a 5-weight fly rod, it seems plenty big enough.

The trout were the normal mix of rainbows, browns, and the occasional little brook trout: the usual suspects in water that's been planted off and on for over half a century, sometimes with a management plan in mind, other times just with whatever was available. The biggest fish were rainbows, and I asked our guide, Jim, about them. He said the place manages for the wildest trout possible, but does do some "supplemental stocking" to keep the fish sizes and numbers where they want them, which you suspect is slightly more than the river would produce on its own. If you're really curious about the extent to which your fishing experience has been shrink-wrapped, you can always ask, but it's usually easy enough to figure out, since wild trout are to hatchery fish as ruffed grouse are to Kentucky Fried Chicken.

All our mornings began the same way. Breakfast was at seven, but coffee was on at six, so I'd leave the cabin at five forty-five for the ten-minute walk to the lodge, where I'd stand with an empty cup watching the last few drops dribble into the pot. I'd set an alarm but I never needed it, because C.D.'s sneaking out early would always wake me, even though he was trying hard not to. He'd found a bend in the river right behind the cabin that he wanted to paint, but the light was right only for a short time, so he had to be there before dawn. These were cold mornings, with horses in the pasture blowing clouds of steam, and I want to say he was working in fingerless gloves, but I can't actually recall that. (Remember, this was before coffee.) C.D. would sometimes show up a little late for breakfast, and if someone said something like, "Hey, sleepyhead, glad you could join us," he wouldn't mention that he'd been up working for two hours.

After breakfast we'd start out fishing together with Jim, either leapfrogging up the stream or taking turns on the pools. C.D. is a good fisherman and a stylish caster who never gave any indication of being distracted, but he must have been, because now and then he'd excuse himself for an hour or so to paint. He carried the slickest painting kit in a medium-sized backpack: paints and brushes for both watercolors and oils, watercolor paper and small stretched canvases, homemade drying boxes (the store-bought kind are too heavy), various other necessary odds and ends, and of course a collapsible easel and a small sunshade that looked like a miniature black umbrella. Watching him unpack and set up reminded me of that old circus gag in which more clowns than you can believe pile out of a tiny little car.

There were fish in this small water of twenty inches, plus or minus—sometimes plus a lot—and I hooked and landed some and lost others that had obviously memorized every exposed root and stump in their pools. (Big lost fish were a constant topic at dinner.) One really nice rainbow took a size-16 Quill Gordon in an eddy at the head of a run—right where Jim said he'd be—shook his head once, and ran forty yards straight downstream to a sunken root ball, where he deftly broke me off. Okay, fair enough, but then two days later at the same spot, Jim put me back on the same eddy, and when the fish made his run, Jim waded into the water and spooked him back up to the head of the pool, where we could play him out and net him. I briefly wondered if that was entirely fair, then decided that all fish caught by a guided fisherman are the result of a team effort; it's just that this effort was more obvious than most.

After dinner at the lodge I'd hang around with the other guests long enough to avoid being rude, then walk back to the cabin and take the chill off with a little fire in the woodstove. Then I'd sit on the porch thinking things over and listening to the resident bull moose shuffling and breathing in the darkness.

My sister and I had already agreed that if we were in the same shape Mom was in at the end—in pain and with advancing dementia—we'd have been tired of it and ready to go. Of course, countless survivors have said the same thing countless times before, and you can never know for sure, but that's what we thought. I remembered when the hardest-working man I've ever known dropped dead on the job and people said, "It's the way Herb would have wanted to go," when in fact it was the way *we* wanted him to go. For all we know, Herb might have preferred a beach in Mazatlán.

I reminded my sister of the time Mom wanted to talk to me about her "estate," which wasn't all that much even then.

I said, "Nothing would make me happier than to learn you'd spent your last dollar on the day you died."

She said, "That's funny—that's exactly what your sister said," and it seemed to please her. Of course, in my ignorance I pictured the money going for cruises and wine-soaked lunches with friends instead of the doctors and nursing homes where most of it eventually went.

After a certain point everyone's life is informed by loss. It's not surprising, but it's still a surprise. The permanence of it feels like a life sentence, and there's always an echo of selfish regret: if there was anything that could have been made right, it's too late now, and it always will be. And the oddly practical question of "What now?" arises. For one thing, Mom now joined the growing number of dead people in my address book whose names I don't have the heart to cross out and who may eventually come to outnumber the living. For another, there are still those two categories of things that your mother must

94

never know and small victories and accomplishments that she'd enjoy hearing about, except they're now both moot.

And there's the odd way memories sink in one place as the initial sting wears off and then resurface unexpectedly somewhere else. I think of some of the people I've lost every day, while others hardly ever come to mind, and it has nothing to do with how often I saw them, how much I liked them, or how many years have passed. The same goes for the animals I've lived with. Some of my old dogs and cats seem to have closed the books and moved on, but I can't shake the feeling that my favorite tomcat is still hanging around the place, hunting ghost rodents and napping invisibly in the sun.

C.D.'s paintings predictably appeared on the mantel in the dining room: first the watercolors that were each done in a single sitting, and then later the oils that took days to complete—one of the bend in the river behind the cabin at first light, the other of the fishy pool under a decrepit wooden bridge farther downstream, where I never did manage to hook a trout. The sunrise felt serene while mercifully falling short of being inspirational, and the bridge—my favorite of the two—had an understated brooding quality, but don't ask me how either effect was achieved. Presumably fishermen could later be added to any of these, but as they stood they were entirely realized unpeopled landscapes that I won't try to further describe in print except to say that the same friend who pointed out C.D.'s resemblance to Clark Kent called him "a sporting man's Monet."

The few times I've asked, C.D. has explained to me in detail what he's doing in terms of the relative values of colors, how diminishing detail is used to suggest receding space, or how the intricacies of composition keep your eye within the frame. I understood the techniques, but not how they rose above being exercises in craft to become works of art. We've also talked about our respective work habits, which in his case seem to be composed of roughly equal parts compulsion, self-indulgence, and good old American work ethic. But on a couple of trips where we've traveled, fished, and roomed together, I've never heard him say anything the least bit lofty or philosophical about art. Like other artists I've talked to—not to mention actors, musicians, writers, and many fishermen—C.D. seems to have long since left considerations of why behind and is now entirely engrossed in how. He simply does the work, puts it away, and then goes fishing.

But the one thing C.D. *is* adamant about is the efficacy of plein air painting: working outside, on-site, with natural light shining on actual objects. He doesn't see how you could get it right any other way, and when he puts it like that he's entirely convincing, but of course others do it differently. One of my favorite paintings, by my friend Bob White, was done in his studio several years ago based on a series of photos I sent him of a place he's never been. The scene is of C.D. himself painting in the rain on a remote river in Labrador under the shelter of a plastic tarp, which Bob wisely changed from its original toxic-waste green to brown.

Sentiment keeps me from being an objective critic here. I'm too enamored with the idea of one artist I like working in a studio in Minnesota depicting another artist I like working out in the weather in northeast Canada with little old me and my waterproof digital camera as the go-between. Still, I'll go out on a limb and say process is crucial to the individual artist, as it should be, but in the grand scheme it doesn't matter how you did it as long as you got it right.

The funeral back in Missouri went as expected. There was the short, vaguely religious service; the church basement lunch of midwestern comfort food, with all of us looking slightly uncomfortable in clothes we otherwise never wear; the often repeated family stories that change a little with each retelling; and the predictable examples of small-town wisdom, as when a cousin said, "Burying your mother is no fun, but at least it's a chore you only have to do once."

And then someone put a hand on my shoulder and asked, "So, where are you going fishing next?"

11.

FOOL'S ERRAND

In mid-August we flew to the headwaters of the George River at Lake Juliette, just over the Labrador border into eastern Quebec, and launched a pair of twenty-foot fiberglass canoes. As far as we knew, we'd be only the fourth party ever to canoe this part of the river. The first two were the Mina Hubbard and Dillon Wallace expeditions way back in 1905. Both groups crossed Labrador using slightly different routes, portaged over a low rise of land into the headwaters of the George in Quebec, and then floated some 350 miles north to a trading post on Ungava Bay. That was two years after Mina's husband, Leonidas, died of starvation and exposure before reaching the George on his party's failed 1903 attempt. Then, in 2003, another group mounted a successful fifty-day, 650-mile canoe trip to commemorate the Leonidas Hubbard expedition that had gone so wrong a hundred years earlier.

As far as we knew, that was it. People do occasionally canoe the George, but they paddle down the de Pas River from Schefferville to Indian House Lake (or Lac de la Hutte Sauvage) and then follow the bigger water on to Ungava Bay, bypassing over a hundred miles of the headwaters we had our eye on.

But we weren't out to do that kind of heroic paddling; we were just interested in the fishing. We assumed there'd be brook trout in the upper George because they were known to be in the lower river, although we didn't know how big they'd be, and we thought that by August some landlocked salmon might have migrated that far upriver. Either way, it was doubtful any fish in that stretch had seen an artificial fly in its lifetime.

There were six of us. Carter Davidson, the filmmaker from Maine, was there to shoot a documentary on landlocked salmon.

Aimee Eaton is a fishing and nature writer from Colorado who said she didn't even know where Labrador was when she got Carter's call.

Simon Guay is a French-Canadian fishing guide who knows as much as anyone about brook trout and salmon, but freely admits that northern pike are his favorite fish.

John Reitman is an ex-military man who's so vague about his time in the service that you suspect he was ordered not to talk about it. He said his personal motto is "semper Gumby" (always flexible), and he'd brought along two things you should have on this kind of trip but hope you won't need: a first-aid kit extensive enough to do minor surgery, and a big-bore rifle.

Robin Reeve owns Three Rivers Lodge in Labrador—our jumping-off spot for Lake Juliette. I've known him longest and best, and one thing I know is that he has a penchant for scouting trips that are supposedly aimed at opening new water for the lodge but that invariably turn out to be too complicated and expensive to dollar up with clients. I think he just wants an excuse to fish new rivers, but I've never asked him about it for fear he won't invite me on any more of these fool's errands.

And then there was me, in my capacity as editor-at-large for *Fly Rod & Reel* magazine: a more or less honorary title I secretly like, because I think the phrase "at large" makes me sound dangerous.

For a while it looked like this trip wouldn't happen. By the time we got to the lodge, southwestern Labrador was socked in with cold wind, continuous rain, and a ceiling that seemed to lower by the hour without ever quite reaching the ground. Good weather for poking a fire in the woodstove and sipping coffee; not so good for wilderness canoeing and camping, let alone getting to the river by floatplane in the first place.

We chanced a shorter flight to Indian Rapids, a wide, riffly channel between two lakes that Robin said might or might not hold brook trout or landlocked salmon. This late in the season both species are migrating upstream to spawn, and their whereabouts in these vast, complicated drainages aren't easy to predict. We landed a five-pound and a six-pound brook trout and lost a third, but there were no salmon.

Day two was dark, raining hard, and chilly enough to see your breath, but not quite cold enough to put off the intrepid Labrador mosquitoes and blackflies. We flew one drainage west to the McKenzie River, where a lodge owner Robin knew had no fishermen in that week and said he'd help us look for salmon.

We hiked two miles downriver in a steady rain on a trail that was several inches deep in standing water and used the boat that was stashed down there to ferry across a small lake. At the outlet Aimee hooked a salmon that jumped once and came off, and in the river downstream Robin hooked and landed a fat salmon of about eight pounds. Those fish cheered Carter up considerably, but they were the only ones we found.

On the way back we saw a large bear turd next to the trail that hadn't been there on the hike down a few hours earlier. The bear had obviously been feasting on blueberries, because this turd was not only bigger than average, it was the most surprising shade of purple. Carter stopped to take several close-up photos of it. No one asked why.

Back at the camp, wind and rain were howling across the lake, visibility was down to a quarter mile, and our pilot, Gilles Morin, said we'd be unable to fly back. We sat in the kitchen at the empty lodge drinking coffee strong enough to warp a spoon while the owner said he could feed us "something out of cans" for supper and that we were welcome to his vacant bunks. We were just settling in to the idea of staying the night when Gilles came in from checking the plane for the third time. He didn't like the way the waves were slamming the pontoons against the dock, but there was no sheltered place to tie up, so he thought we should "try to make it back" before dark.

We took off into cloud cover low enough to obscure the treetops, but by staying under the low overcast we could see well enough to bank around the hills and feel our way back to Three Rivers, wiping the condensation off the inside of the windshield with a canvas work glove. We were flying in a small plane in weather that would make me think twice about driving my Jeep, but I'd flown with Gilles on previous trips and shared Robin's confidence in him. He's a small, precise man in a leather jacket and baggy hip boots; not at all shy, but not overly talkative, either, with an uncanny sense of weather and a reputation as a pilot who can perform borderline miraculous feats with a de Havilland Beaver.

The whole George River plan depended on Gilles. The common wisdom was that once you pushed off from Lake Juliette, you'd have to go something like fifty or sixty miles before coming to a place where any sane pilot could land to pick you up. Above that, the river itself was too narrow and serpentine, and although there were some pond-like wide spots that looked promising on the map, Gilles had scouted them from the air and said they were too shallow and rocky. But he *had* located a stretch of river that was wide enough, deep enough, and just long enough to land a floatplane—and, more important, take off again with a payload.

Had he actually done this, or had he just scoped it out from the air? At times a slight language barrier kicks in with Gilles. He speaks some English, but his first language is French, and the only French I have is what I've picked up from the multilingual signage in Montreal and Quebec City. I can say "exit" and "napkin" and "thank you," which is not the stuff of nuanced conversation. For his part, Gilles sometimes falls back on one of those eloquent shrugs the French have perfected—a shrug that in this case seemed to say, "Having actually done it and just knowing I *can* do it amount to the same thing."

We had a meeting the morning of day three. We didn't have unlimited time to wait for conditions to change, but there was the question of whether we could fly to the George in this weather, and even if we could, none of us was anxious to rush into a survival situation. Someone pointed out that there are two ways to get hypothermia on a canoe trip in the rain: gradually or suddenly.

We made a quick hop out to Rick's—not to be confused with Middle Rick's, Upper Rick's, or Rick's Surprise. This was a small, steep, alder-choked channel between lakes that reminded me of a creek in the Rocky Mountains, except that the brook trout there weighed between one and a half and two pounds. These aren't impressive fish for Labrador, but Aimee said she couldn't bring herself to think of a two-pound brook trout as "small." Neither could I.

At the inlet to the next lake I hooked something heavy on a weighted streamer, and Carter filmed while the fish ran me out into the backing and spit the hook. Carter said it must have been a lake trout or a pike, because a salmon would have jumped.

On the morning of day four the weather broke chilly and bright with high, soggy-looking clouds in a blue sky, so we hustled our gear together and flew to Lake Juliette. It took three long trips: one with the canoes—which have to be strapped to the pontoon struts, where they cause aerodynamic problems—another with gear and provisions, and a third with the fishermen. Then there was the painstaking business of distributing and balancing the loads in the canoes and the required group photo that Carter insisted on taking so he wouldn't have to be in it. (For a filmmaker, he's oddly camera shy.)

The George began unspectacularly, spilling out of the lake into a wide, bumpy riffle that was so unreadable we simply entered it at random, steering around visible rocks, watching for deadheads, and getting a sense of how these boats handled, which wasn't well. Even empty the big canoes weren't exactly nimble, and loaded down with gear and fishermen they felt waterlogged and unresponsive.

The river flowed placidly through flat country left behind by the last ice age, but now and then there'd be enough of a drop to create rapids that we'd either run or walk the canoes down. At the bottom of these there'd be a fan of current spreading into deeper water, and that's where we got into brook trout: big ones of four to six pounds at the lip of the rapids, and smaller ones of a pound or so above that in the pockets. Not a lot—a few at each spot at best—but fat, wild, beautiful, innocent fish.

Simon, Robin, and I were paddling downriver toward one of these spots—rubbernecking at the fishy water below—when we abruptly got sideways in the rapids. I'm not sure how it happened. At first it looked like we'd taken a good line, and then it didn't. All I clearly remember is John's worried, helpless look from the other canoe as he tried to work out how to help and couldn't come up with anything. In the end, we managed to keep the canoe from capsizing, but we lost a paddle. No harm done, since we had a spare, and anyway things had gotten a little dreamy by then, and it was a useful reminder that a river will purr like a kitten if you pet it right, but it's still an unpredictable animal that's capable of anything.

We camped in wet woods with a floor of lichens and caribou moss that had the consistency of a damp sponge and looked like it should be growing in a petri dish. We pitched the tents far away from where we cooked and roped the provision boxes up in trees in case the food smells attracted a bear. They say this region is lousy with bears— hence John's rifle—but then, no one ever comes here, so how would they know? In fact, this was inhospitable country without much to eat, and so wildlife was scarce. In our entire time on the river I saw exactly two ravens, one boreal chickadee, and one golden eagle. That's it. We never saw a mammal of any kind—not the bear, moose, or caribou you'd expect in northern wilderness; not even a squirrel.

I had an old pocket watch in my gear, but didn't see any point in winding it, so it eventually stopped. (I don't mean that metaphorically; there was just no reason to worry about what time it was. The same thing sometimes happens at home.) Meanwhile the landscape unrolled, with its stunted black spruce, spindly tamarack, and muskeg where our footprints sprang back almost as soon as we made them. It was so quiet away from the rapids that even a pretty little riffle around the next bend sounded like Victoria Falls. This landscape was exactly how it's always been and how it's supposed to be: a place where you can experience the peculiarly modern pleasure of being pretty sure you're not under surveillance.

The fishing was good, but no better than in places that were much easier and cheaper to get to; the trees were too small for lumber, the scenery was unspectacular, and no minerals worth extracting had been found. This wasn't designated wilderness but wilderness by default: a remote northern region where no one had yet figured out how to make a buck.

I remembered that E. Donnall Thomas Jr. once wrote, "It is shocking to realize that our greatest accomplishment as a species may be to escape all traces of ourselves." That made me think of poor Leonidas Hubbard, who was so eager to make his mark in the waning days of the era of exploration. He believed the region would be teeming with enough game to feed his party and realized only by degrees that he was wrong. If he'd made it this far, there might have been the ancestors of these fat brook trout to eat, but as it was, he escaped all traces of his species, and his last meal consisted of his moccasins, or so the story goes.

The woods were so wet that we ended up living in our waders except while we were sleeping—pulling them on in lieu of pants every morning—and even then by day two everything was clammy. Even the spruce twigs we broke off for kindling were rubbery with moisture and draped in the greenish-gray lichen known as witch's hair, so our fires tended toward the smoky side.

With six of us in camp, the chores went quickly. The last thing each night was to boil a big pot of water that we'd use to fill our canteens the next morning—except for Robin, who drank straight from the river out of habit. It was probably safe, but the rest of us had all had giardia at least once and didn't want to get it again, especially out here. Whatever wilderness epiphany I might have hoped for arrived in just those kinds of practical terms: this was no place to dump a canoe, twist an ankle, or get the Hershey squirts.

Carter filmed it all diligently but unobtrusively, without making us feel we were on a movie set, although I suppose technically we were. He never seemed disappointed that none of these fish were the landlocked salmon he and his sponsors were hoping for, although he sometimes wore the thoughtful expression of a man who was rethinking a project on the run. Every documentarian knows there can be more than one true story in any sequence of events, and this was beginning to look like a story about brook trout.

And why not? These north-country fish are just handsomer than other brook trout—especially in August when they're fat from a short growing season and colored up for the spawn—and they're uniformly bigger than they get anywhere else. It's a function of inhabiting the northernmost end of their native range, where they live long, hard lives in conditions that would kill lesser fish. They can be hard to find, and once you find them you usually won't catch very many, which only makes the ones you do catch more vivid. I've been coming to this region on and off for twenty years now for the simple reason that I don't know what I'd do without these beautiful brook trout.

One day I was perched on a rock at the bottom of wide, stair-step rapids fishing a streamer on a sink-tip line. I was casting parallel to the rapids, stripping back through the broken water, and then working out in a fan pattern into deeper current braided by sunken boulders. It all looked fishy as hell, and I couldn't imagine any brook trout in here being able to resist my size-4 Red Ghost, so I wanted to make sure they all had a chance to see it. When I got a take I set hard and saw a thick flash of orange as the fish rolled. I played it carefully—maybe even timidly. I'd lost a good one earlier by getting impatient and trying to rush it to the net, and none of us were catching so many that we could easily shrug off a blown chance.

These fish aren't flashy fighters—there are no jumps or long, reel-screaming runs—but they're muscular and dogged and put up an awful commotion when they're hooked. It's hard to describe the physics and tactics of landing a fish beyond John Casey's admonition that "when the fish does something, you do nothing, and when the fish does nothing, you do something," but it's fair to say that if you play it too hard, you'll lose it, and you'll also lose it if you don't play it hard enough. There are those who say they fish to relax, but how can you relax when there's so much at stake?

Finally Simon dipped up the perfect brook trout in his long-handled net. It was a six-pound male built like a cinder block with a humped back, wide shoulders, and hard gut, wearing his best orange spawning colors. This was a prosperous fish in his prime, and if he had a thought in his head, it was only to pass on his blue-ribbon genes. After I released him, Simon shook my hand as if I'd just won a Pulitzer Prize, which is more or less how I felt.

We got in a little fishing on our last morning, but had to get back early to break camp before the plane arrived. Carter, Aimee, Robin, and I went out first, along with some of the gear, while John and Simon stayed to finish packing. Once we'd loaded up, Gilles taxied so far upstream that when he swung the plane around, the rudders of the pontoons barely cleared the rocks at the bottom of the next riffle. As soon as we were facing downstream he pushed the throttle all the way forward and the plane roared and lurched. I didn't see how this could work. A floatplane needs a certain minimum amount of room to get airborne (more than it takes to land; even more with a load on board), and the black spruce woods at the next bend were too tall and entirely too close. I wished I'd cleared up the question of whether Gilles had actually done this before or just *thought* he could do it. I wondered whether John and Simon had sent us out first just to see if we'd make it.

By the time the pontoons came off the water the trees had filled the windshield, and we weren't gaining altitude fast enough to clear the crowns. Given time to think it over I might have concluded that this was a better place than most to check out, but in the moment I just thought it was all happening too fast. I'd just braced for impact when Gilles banked hard to the right, flying sideways below the treetops around the sharp bend in the river with one wing nearly cutting a wake in the water until he had room to level off and climb out. It was all in a day's work for a bush pilot Carter would later describe as "ninety-nine percent business and one percent crazy," and even before I managed to swallow the lump in my throat, I was happier than I'd ever been to be alive and in the air.

12.

YOU CAN'T EAT THE SCENERY

Someone had spray-painted "Rehab is for quitters" on an otherwise blank concrete wall. This was in the Designated Smoking Area outside the Anchorage Airport where I was waiting out the third consecutive delay of my flight with some strong, silent types I took to be commercial fishermen. (Roughnecks from the oilfields have a more sullen look, and everyone else dresses better.) Flight delays are so common in Alaska that waiting gracefully becomes a necessary skill, and since it's done in public, there's an element of performance to it.

I try to imagine myself as a character actor—maybe a Bruce Dern type—playing the role of the veteran north-country traveler who understands that no amount of fretting and whining will make the plane go if the plane isn't going. Meanwhile, the real old hands simply find a patch of unoccupied floor and lie down for a nap, hugging their backpacks as though they were feather pillows.

The flight was finally called three hours late, and my friend Ed and I walked out onto the tarmac with a dozen other sports and climbed aboard the little turboprop Saab 340. We fastened our seat belts, they started the engines, and we waited for the plane to move. A few minutes later the engines sputtered to a stop and the pilot came out and asked if we'd please go back inside and wait in the terminal. He did say "please," but it wasn't a request.

From inside, several of us watched as a guy pulled up in a van, climbed a stepladder, and began tinkering with the starboard engine. (Work of this kind is deeply fascinating when it's being done on a plane you're about to fly in.) Sometime later he replaced the cowling, the pilot restarted the engine, and they both stood a little distance away talking. I couldn't help but imagine the conversation:

There. How's that sound?

Sounds like a weed whacker; you expect me to fly that thing?

We got back on board, and this time the plane taxied smartly out to the runway. I don't have more than the usual fear of flying, but I did hope the aircraft would work this time and that to a trained ear both engines would sound more like Maseratis than weed whackers.

Soon we were at altitude and flying southwest toward Bristol Bay. Off the left side of the plane a river poured through a canyon into the Gulf of Alaska. Off to the right its corrugated headwaters reached to the horizon with blue-green glaciers nestled in their cirques. Only minutes by air from the biggest city in the state, and already the landscape seemed unimaginably somber and remote.

When the guy in the seat ahead of me came back from the bathroom, he said to his seatmate, "That toilet is so small I ended up pissing in my hat by mistake."

At the lodge we suited up and motored down Aleknagik Lake to the mouth of the Agulowak River with these ancient Athabaskan names catching in our throats like chicken bones. At this time of year—mid-July—three- to four-inch-long sockeye salmon smolts pour out of the river by the tens of thousands on their way to salt water, and Arctic char and Dolly Vardens stack up there to ambush them. It's a perfect setup for fish and fishermen.

When we came around the last point we could see it was in full swing. There were half a dozen other boats anchored or drifting near the mouth—two that we recognized from the lodge, the rest probably up from Dillingham—and the air was filled with wheeling and diving Arctic terns, while fat white gulls bobbed around like anchored yachts. Fish were milling all over, but every few minutes a pod of char would push a school of smolts to the surface and a quarter acre of fish would boil past the anchored boat at current speed. When one of these frenzies went into a window in the glare you could see it all clearly: hundreds of silver smolts flashing like welding sparks in the sun, and uncountable ominous shapes looming up from below like something from a painting by Hieronymus Bosch.

The Agulowak is a big river, so multiply that by a current plume hundreds of yards wide and a quarter mile long, where seven boats are spaced far enough apart to avoid tangling lines even on long runs, and in each boat there's at least one fisherman holding a bent rod. This is the kind of jaw-dropping abundance that draws fishermen to Alaska and that also sometimes produces cases of shameful fish hoggery. I don't mean the locals who diligently fill freezers with fillets because winters here are as certain as death and taxes; I'm talking about dentists from Omaha who lug home coffin-sized coolers of fish that their wives won't know what to do with. A few big meals where Dad brays about being the hunter-gatherer back from the wilderness, and the rest is lost to freezer burn.

I once overheard an argument between one of these privileged dimwits and a bush pilot who'd spent one too many seasons watching the pointless carnage.

"Why shouldn't I bring home fifty pounds of salmon? They're gonna die anyway."

"They're gonna die *after they spawn*, and every one you kill is one more that doesn't. Are you really too stupid to see that, or are you just playing dumb so you can go on being an asshole?"

The next day we flew out to a compact little tent camp on the Togiak River: a couple of WeatherPorts pitched on an open coastal floodplain with a fire pit and improvised driftwood lawn furniture out front. There we were told that the king salmon fishing had been "slow": a fisherman's euphemism for "pointless." For weeks now the weather had been sunny and warm for Alaska, and a lack of rain had kept the Togiak and other rivers in the region low and on the warm side. Some said the kings had petered through early—a few at a time, but never in fishable numbers—and were now far upriver spawning. Others thought the few that had been seen were advance scouts and that the bulk of the run was still staged in salt water, waiting for gray skies and a flush of water. Less analytical types just thought it was a rotten year for kings.

Our guide, Taylor, said chums were a better bet. Most were already in and spawning, but there were still plenty of stragglers we could fish to. And of course the Dollys were almost a sure thing. They'd be staged just downstream of the spawning chums picking up stray eggs, and would be pushovers for orange plastic beads. Ed and I exchanged a look and said we'd like to try for kings.

The run Taylor took us to had a sloping pea-gravel bottom dropping into a slot where the current ran smooth, deep, and deceptively fast against a far bank lined with black cottonwoods. This is where the kings would be. Taylor had seen them there as recently as the day before, but said they "weren't doing anything." I looped the heaviest sink-tip I had onto my Skagit head, dug out a five-inch-long Intruder fly I'd slaved over the previous winter, and asked Taylor what he thought of it. He said, "Yeah, that could work," with the guide's typical emphasis on "could."

Ed and I fished through the run, casting tight to the far bank and then throwing big, loopy mends to sink the flies as deep as possible before they started to swing. I wasn't sure I was getting deep enough, but I couldn't think of how else to do it. When Taylor waded in and stood off my left shoulder, I said, "I'm open to suggestions here."

He said, "Yer fishin' it like I would."

He was handling us. We were here only for the day and we wanted to do the one thing that wasn't going to work, so rather than trying to talk us out of it, he was letting us knock on this door until it was obvious even to us that no one was home.

When we felt we'd given it our best, we piled into the johnboat and drifted over the run to have a look. The salmon were podded up right on the bottom in the gut of the run, six or seven of them, startlingly big and motionless as logs. Fish like these are said to be "sulking," as if they're not just uninterested in your fly but are punishing you for some perceived insult and refuse to bite out of sheer peevishness.

Without saying "I told you so," Taylor then took us to two other pools where chums were rolling in the hard current, and we caught some. These fish usually come in third in the Pacific salmon sweepstakes, after kings for their size and silvers for their numbers and aggressiveness. Chums aren't classically pretty salmon by a long shot, but they wear their snaggle-toothed homeliness with style, bite a fly angrily, and fight like wolverines. So what's not to love?

Late that afternoon we flew to Birch Creek Camp. As we humped our gear up from the plane, I asked one of the guides, Jason, why it was called that, since it was actually on the Middle Fork of the Goodnews River. He said the name dates to the early days of the lodge, when the original owners were scouting locations. They didn't want anyone who might be eavesdropping on their radio chatter to know where they were fishing, so they made up fictitious names for the rivers. I pushed my luck and asked, "What was the news that was so good it has a river named after it?" He didn't know.

Ed went off with Eric, the other guide, to catch some Dollys before dinner, while I sat in a folding chair in front of my tent to untangle my backing. On the last pool on the Togiak I'd foul-hooked a large chum right ahead of the dorsal fin, giving it extra leverage and making Taylor and me think it was a big king. We chased it in the boat, and in the ensuing confusion I managed to repeatedly wind my line and backing onto the reel in sloppy overlapping loops that then cinched themselves into a seemingly endless series of world-class granny knots each time I came tight to the fish. I could have put away the spey rod and fished a one-hander for Dollys at Birch Creek, but I've become a stickler for keeping my tackle in order, because some of the slapstick routines from the days when I didn't are still vividly painful memories.

By the time Ed and Eric got back I'd finished my chore and was relaxing, watching the wakes of chum salmon running up the riffle in front of camp and wondering if untangling backing for eternity would be my job in hell. When Ed walked up from the boat, I asked, "How'd it go?"

"We just now came around a bend tight to the bank and almost bumped into a sow brown bear with a cub," he said. "They were *really close.*"

"How close?" I asked.

He said, "If they'd jumped one way instead of the other, they'd have ended up in the boat."

Ed was still wide-eyed with adrenaline, and I knew the feeling. All tourists love to see bears at the kind of respectful distance that mimics a TV screen, but it's the sudden, close-range encounters that reveal these animals for what they are: not so much romantic icons of wilderness as six-hundred-pound meat grinders.

As an afterthought, Ed added, "We caught a shitload of fish."

We spent the next day catching Dollys and rainbows on beads and flesh flies. On my first trip to Alaska I had to get used to the idea of these noble game fish gorging on stray salmon eggs and shreds of rotting flesh as a succession of five species of Pacific salmon run up the rivers to spawn, die, and decompose—not to mention fishing flies tied with sickly pinkish-beige rabbit fur intended to imitate rancid meat. It's one thing to be told that the entire ecosystem here depends on countless tons of dead salmon and that without those nutrients brought inland from the ocean every year, Alaska would be a cold, fishless desert, but once you actually see it you realize that this is the aquatic version of fifty million buffalo.

The most striking example I ever saw was one September on the Karluk River on Kodiak Island. Miles of riverbank to the high-water line were ankle-deep and slippery with the corpses of pink, sock-eye, and silver salmon, and the river itself looked and smelled like a cauldron of spoiled cioppino. Kodiak bears the size of pickup trucks were greasy with fish oil and so stuffed with salmon they could hardly move. Likewise, the big, sleek Dolly Vardens in from Uyak Bay were so full of salmon eggs they were dribbling them out their gill covers. If you've ever fished with dead drift nymphs, beads will be a familiar form of manipulation, but these fish would chase a bead even on a swing, apparently so blinded by gluttony that it didn't occur to them that eggs don't swim. This is the best reason to go to Alaska: not for the chance at fifty-fish days but to see for yourself that nature isn't the least bit dainty or sentimental.

We had a good day on the Agulupak River, where we caught

rainbows and big, pretty graylings on dry flies with my old friend Bob White and had one of his famous shore lunches of fresh sockeye salmon, fried potatoes, and the breaded and fried green apple slices known as "guide pie." Ed and I ate as if we hadn't seen food in a week, while Bob nibbled on a single piece of fish. "If I ate like that every day," he said, nodding at my second tin plate of fried fish and potatoes, "I'd weigh three hundred pounds."

Bob is a successful artist with a serious guiding habit who can't seem to stay away from Alaska. He's been guiding for a long time and looks it, with windburned cheeks and a beard like steel wool. I don't know if he has actual seniority at the lodge (the pecking order isn't obvious to outsiders), but the other guides look up to him as an elder statesman and role model. When one young guy made a shore lunch that was almost an exact copy of Bob's and I asked him about it, he said, "You quickly figure out that however Bob does it is the way it should be done."

The fishing was dead at Rainbow Camp—another example of forty-year-old misdirection—where we arrived on the downside of the boom-and-bust cycle. The kings weren't there for reasons that were open to discussion, and the chums were spawning farther up the small river than we could get by boat, with the Dollys and most of the rainbows right behind them.

We motored upriver anyway to see what we could find, slowing in one pool to miss the single handlebar of a snowmobile that was protruding just above the surface. It hadn't been there when I'd fished the river the year before, and Matt and Tyler said they didn't know the story behind it, although it's hard to imagine a scenario set in an Alaskan winter that starts with a snowmobiler going through the ice miles from the nearest settlement and ends happily. They said they'd kept an eye out for a body for the first few weeks in camp and then pretty much forgot about it.

We swung a few deep pools to see if maybe an errant king salmon was around, but mostly because we needed something to do, since we all understood that nothing much would happen here until the silver salmon arrived in a few weeks. It would have been a good day for a boat ride, some bird-watching, and a leisurely lunch, but guides hate to send their clients away skunked, so Matt found a pair of spawned-out chums and put Ed into a couple of rainbows staged below them that ate a flesh fly. And later I got a rainbow on a mouse pattern by following Tyler's detailed instructions. He called the strike so accurately that I had to suspect this was the camp pet, usually reserved for children and beginners. Nice fish, though.

It was hot enough on the flight back to the lodge that we flew with the windows of the Beaver open, enhancing the illusion that these things are just flying pickup trucks. While we were still climbing I saw two bald eagles sitting on a rock at the top of a hill looking up at us with obvious disdain. Later there was a pair of white trumpeter swans posing on an emerald pond like ornamental swans on an English estate, and farther on there were a bull moose with giant antlers and several tributary creeks running red with sockeye salmon.

There's a lot to be said for these lodges that operate on the grand-tour model. For one thing, you see six or seven rivers at close range and lots more beautifully empty country in between from a float-plane, which incidentally fulfills a childhood fantasy of mine sparked by overwrought stories in *Field & Stream*. Also, when the fishing sucks—as it occasionally does—you know you'll be somewhere else tomorrow where it will probably be better. The flip side is that when the fishing is fabulous, you know you'll be leaving on the same plane that brings in your replacements, so it's possible to begin getting nostalgic by lunchtime. And as the trip winds down there can be the sneaking suspicion that although you saw multiple rivers and caught countless fish, you never quite sank your teeth into anything.

This can make you mildly jealous of the guides who work there and live what seem like enviably authentic lives at the camps you only visit for a day. Still, you avoid gazing around admiringly and saying, "God, what a place to spend the summer!" because the guy's heard it a hundred times and might reply, *Yeah, well, you can't eat the scenery.* There's sometimes a fundamental disconnect between guides in their twenties and thirties and clients at the deep end of middle age. This can be as complicated as fathers and sons or as simple as the fact that, as Gina Ochsner put it, "Young men drink because they don't know who they are, and old men drink because they do."

On our last day we ended up back at the mouth of the Agulowak, fishing for the same char and Dollys that were plenty big and fat a week before but that were now fatter and a couple of inches longer on average. That was hard to believe, until I considered the staggering amount of protein that changes hands in these transactions: enough that you could actually see the fish had grown in a week's time.

We were casting across and down current, fishing a slow swing with any streamer fly that was large and predominantly white. Intuition said to strip fast to mimic the panicked prey, but we'd learned all that would get you was foul-hooked fish; there were that many char in the water. I said I thought the fish were taking our slowly drifting streamers for stunned or injured smolts and got noncommittal shrugs from Ed and our guide, who both understood that when fish are gorging like this it doesn't matter *what* your fly is doing as long as it's in the water.

We were back at the lodge early, taking hot showers and packing up for the flight out in the morning. Anglers travel a long way to find a seemingly inexhaustible supply of big, wild, gullible fish, but unless you're trying to feed a village for the winter, there's no reason to catch a boatload. After five fish in a row you can say you've figured it out; at ten you've made your point; and somewhere short of twenty a sense of unease develops that could easily blossom into embarrassment. The trick is to enjoy the spectacle and then quit while it's still fun.

13.

CAMP FOOD

In Ernest Hemingway's 1925 short story "Big Two-Hearted River," the protagonist, Nick, sets up camp after a long hike with a heavy pack that makes him desperately hungry. So before he goes fishing, he cooks a reckless meal: he mixes a can of pork and beans with a can of spaghetti and slathers the whole mess with ketchup. He says to himself, "I've got a right to eat this kind of stuff, if I'm willing to carry it," something every backpacker who's ever lugged cans of food miles into the woods has thought.

Sound familiar? It does to me, right down to the beans and spaghetti with ketchup that would taste better than you think if you were hungry enough. That story was published thirty years before my own first clumsy attempts at childhood fishing and camping, but we were still carrying the same hand-me-down wood-framed canvas packs that weighed as much empty as the later aluminum and nylon jobs would full, not to mention canvas tents with oak poles and steel pegs, metal canteens, cast-iron frying pans, and food in cans weighing just short of a pound each. I remember the midwestern woods and lakes that had to pass as wilderness until we got older. I also remember staggering under brutal loads with unpadded pack straps chewing on my collarbones like angry raccoons. If I hadn't thought that was fun, my course through life might have been different.

Being your own pack animal whets your appetite nicely, so early on I developed a taste for the high-calorie, high-fat canned goods that are now frowned upon by nutritionists—and as the great man said, I felt I deserved it because I'd carried it on my back. (Incidentally, many of the health-food bullies I've met have never hauled anything heavier than a roller bag, and then only from the lobby to the curb.)

Of course, as a child in the 1950s I knew nothing about nutrition; all I knew was what stuck to your ribs, as they used to say. Years later I encountered a food writer who said that if you're eating poorly, you're probably also *living* poorly. That sounded right in theory, but by then I associated eating poorly with the good life, although I did notice that this stuff tasted a lot better cooked over an open fire after a long, strenuous day than it did at the kitchen table.

Didn't our mothers teach us better? Not really, but then, the homegrown, made-from-scratch nostalgia we engage in now was just antique drudgery to them, so when instant mashed potatoes, frozen fish sticks, and TV dinners arrived, they jumped on board, bringing Dad and the kids along for the ride. If you wanted what we'd now call authentic food, you'd have to ride your bike over to Grandma's house.

During my brief career as a Boy Scout I became partial to a certain brand of canned beef stew, with its meat and vegetables packed in glutinous, freakishly orange grease. I didn't last long as a Scout. The regimentation chafed, and I thought I was spending too much time tying knots in church basements and not enough time out in the woods. I finally drifted away, taking with me a lifelong aversion to meetings and a taste for that canned stew that my friends and I were still eating in camp when I turned sixty. We often cooked it right in the can to avoid dirtying an extra pot, but, sadly, you can't do that anymore, because now too many cans come lined with the kind of plastic that gives off carcinogenic gases when it's heated. No wonder we get so sentimental about the old days.

It was only last fall, camping with the old gang on a favorite river in western Colorado, that I began to sense the end of the honeymoon with this beef stew. I'd brought along the largest available can of the stuff (twenty-four ounces) and I offered it up for dinner every night, but the boys always voted it down in favor of something else. So when I broke camp one morning a day ahead of the others, I handed the can to Mike.

"I'll just leave this with you guys," I said.

"Uh, sure, okay . . . ," he replied without enthusiasm.

This is the same guy who once volunteered to bring the food for a weeklong fishing trip and showed up with nothing but a cooked ham, three loaves of bread, and a pound of coffee.

Most of my early camps were simple by choice as well as necessity. My friends and I claimed it was for the sake of traveling light, but the fact is none of us could afford much in the way of gear anyway. We sat on the ground, slept cold, and got wet, and our meals ran to cheap, just-add-water stuff like dried soup, instant rice, and biscuits

made with creek water and the ever-present box of Bisquick. Dehydrated meals for backpackers were available then, but although
they've since improved, the early versions were hideously expensive
and no better than Korean War–surplus C-rations.

And of course, we ate fish, or at least planned to, and for a while
my fly-fishing gear included a secret matchbox containing an assortment of bait hooks and sinkers. I did consider myself to be a
fly-fishing purist, but I also understood that while sport was a matter
of style, collecting protein was an entirely practical business. Worms
and grubs for bait could often be dug on-site, and later in the season
there'd be grasshoppers. They were hard to catch, but if you got out
early enough in the morning while they were still stiff from the cold,
you could pick them off the weed stems like berries.

The ideal of rustic self-sufficiency was big then. Euell Gibbons
was writing about wild edibles, Bradford Angier published books
like *How to Stay Alive in the Woods*, and both left the impression
that a smart outdoorsman could walk into wild country with nothing
but a knife and a book of matches and gain five pounds. It was a nice
thought, but even if you knew what you were doing—and few of us
did—a balanced diet wasn't easy to forage in the Rocky Mountains.

Sometime in the 1970s, three of us backpacked into a high mountain valley filled with beaver ponds, planning to go light and live off
the land. We ate all the trout we could catch, backed up with black
coffee and carefully rationed handfuls from the one small bag of gra-
nola we'd brought. Within forty-eight hours we were suffering from
ketosis, also known as protein starvation. That's where a lack of car-
bohydrates in your diet (exacerbated by exercise) causes your body to
begin consuming itself, starting with stored fat and eventually moving
on to the muscles and vital organs. The sensation is one of constant,
ferocious hunger that not even a dozen beaver ponds filled with nine-
inch brook trout can satisfy.

We stuck it out for four days before hiking out to the car and driving straight to the nearest truck stop. We had pancakes, sausage, and eggs, followed by cheeseburgers and fries. The waitress eyed us suspiciously. We looked a little rough, and she wondered if we had any money to pay for all that food.

For that matter, there were a few fall fishing trips on which I packed my father's old Harrington & Richardson .22 revolver, hoping to bag a stray blue grouse that I would slow-roast over an open fire. But then when the chance came, I emptied all nine shots at the bird without ruffling a feather. It was at that moment that I realized this useless hog leg weighed more than a can of Spam, and that the Spam, though less romantic, was a sure thing.

For some outdoor types, a camp is seen as the open-air equivalent of a good hotel, complete with sumptuous, leisurely meals that can take hours to rustle up. For many fishermen, a camp is simply cheaper than a room and closer to the fishing, and the less time spent fussing with food the better.

We all know stories of the haphazard eating habits of fishermen, like the giant submarine sandwich from the last town that's made to last for days while the bread gets hard, the mayonnaise goes skunky, and the meat turns a metallic green around the edges. And a friend claims that he once fried a brace of trout in a pan greased with fly floatant because he didn't have any oil or bacon drippings. He said it wasn't that bad, but he wouldn't make a habit of it.

A fish camp that's pitched within sight of the pickup—as virtually all of mine are now—allows for luxuries like lawn chairs, two-burner camp stoves, and ample groceries stored in the primitive refrigeration of a cooler, but the laws of physics still apply. Halfway through a warm fall steelhead trip to the Salmon River in Idaho a few years ago, my block of ice melted, my food spoiled, and I had to drive forty miles round-trip to the nearest store for fresh supplies. I missed half a day of fishing, but what really stung was the knowledge that a *real* steelheader would have just chewed some lichen off a rock and kept casting.

Few of my camp food memories actually rise to the level of horror stories. In fact, I don't *have* that many camp food memories. In most cases, I recall the fishing and assume I must have eaten something, because I'd have remembered if I hadn't. Otherwise, it's mostly a matter of breakfasts thrown together carelessly (or skipped altogether because I was in a rush to hit the water) and dinners when I was too tired to do anything but plop a cold wiener in a dry bun and crawl into the sleeping bag. And late in some trips when supplies were running low, there were some improvised burritos that were pretty marginal, but still better than nothing. (In the context of camp cooking, the term "burrito" is taken to mean anything vaguely edible wrapped in a tortilla.)

But then some culinary crimes have risen to the level of tradition, like a friend's signature "sunny-side-up" eggs that are greasy and raw on one side and so burned on the other you have to cut them with a knife. The only time I complained, he said, "Well, you can always go to the café across the street. What? There's no café across the street? Well then maybe you should just eat your eggs and shut the hell up."

For some reason, breakfast is the downfall of many camp cooks. On an Atlantic salmon trip to the coast of Labrador, our bush pilot volunteered to make breakfast one morning while we got our gear together and loaded the canoe. He started out frying a pan full of eggs, but broke too many yolks when he turned them and decided to imperfectly scramble them instead. They ended up looking like an omelet designed by a committee. While he was distracted by the egg problem, the bacon and the toast both burned black. When he served this mess he said, in his picturesque French-Canadian accent, "Remember, I am a better pilot than I am a cook." One member of the party muttered, "God, let's hope."

Sometimes I wonder if there isn't a little posturing in the way some fishermen eat: some rebellious bluster left over from adolescence on the order of "Who needs Mom's home cookin' anyway?" Or maybe it's a remnant of the old he-man mystique whereby men on their own can manage bacon, beans, and coffee, but otherwise don't cook and eventually have to get married to avoid starvation. A friend once wrote in an essay that I was a good camp cook. I was flattered, but I think all he meant was that I was willing to do it. There's an old joke about a fishing camp where the rule is that anyone who complains about the food has to do the cooking himself. One night a guy looks at his plate and says, "This tastes like shit—but it's *good*."

Or maybe it's just that we're all more domesticated than we'd like to think, and sometimes the sudden freedom of a fishing trip makes us as giddy as dogs that have slipped their leashes and are free to eat or roll in anything they can find. For that matter, fresh air, fishing, and exercise generate the kind of hunger that resembles lust, so cold, three-day-old pizza with cardboard stuck to the crust can seem like a feast in the same way that the girls really do get prettier at closing time.

This is all part of the extreme-sport stance where the goal isn't so much to catch some fish as to test the outer limits of your compulsion. So you fish till you're dazed from exhaustion and faint from hunger, thinking that you're straining the last ounce of value out of a trip. It's an approach that makes intuitive sense, and we've all done it, but in fact you'll last longer and fish better if you hit a stride you can maintain and stop now and then to take some nourishment. It's the greenhorn who pushes too hard and hits the wall halfway through a trip, while the old hands fish on at a slower but inexorable pace.

The same goes for drinking. My friends and I—and one friend in particular—used to roll up our sleeves and get shamefully hammered in camp. So much so that once I passed out while blowing on a stubborn campfire and singed off half my beard. I guess it was fun, but I got tired of greeting beautiful morning hatches with a hangover, the shakes, and an empty stomach because I couldn't keep food down. What seemed like morning mist on the river was actually an internal fog that wouldn't burn off till noon, by which time the trout would have stopped rising.

But over the long haul, the head-banging resolved itself into something more sustainable. If nothing else, too much booze and junk food make you feel bad, either right then or eventually. In the short run, this can result in the kind of explosive emergencies that explain the roll of toilet paper stashed in almost everyone's fishing kit. And in the long run, well, who knows? Some fare better than others, but the body's miraculous ability to recover has its limits. Mickey Mantle said: "If I knew I was going to live this long, I'd have taken better care of myself."

Part of this is cultural. We Americans do many things well, but feeding ourselves isn't one of them. Much of our food is poisoned by refined sugar, preservatives, and saturated fats, but health-food snobs are sanctimonious enough to make you long for fast food anyway. We have an obesity rate of nearly 35 percent, while at the same time sixteen million children don't have enough to eat. Meanwhile, government bureaucrats have replaced the word "hunger" with the phrase "food insecurity" in official publications. For the record, food insecurity is worrying that your soufflé will fall; hunger is something else entirely.

But back to camping, where eating well can still be quick and simple as long as you pay minimal attention to ingredients. I think it was Michael Pollan who said, "Even bread and butter can be a great meal if it's really good bread and really good butter." There's no need to get elaborate about it. In fact, camp cooking is best when it's straightforward and unpretentious. Like fly-fishing itself, the essential simplicity of it can easily be smothered under too much equipment and technique.

Once I was in camp with two friends who are good all-around sportsmen and pretty serious foodies. We stopped at a fancy market on the way to the river, where they stocked up on all kinds of fresh, organic, artisanal goodies, and in camp they insisted on doing the cooking because they really were good at it. It naturally fell to me to do the dishes, and there were a lot more of them than I'm used to, including utensils you rarely see in camp, like egg coddlers and garlic presses. (For that matter, my share of the groceries was five times what I usually pay for camp provisions.) I remember in a general way that the food was fabulous, but, oddly, I can't recall a single meal. It's possible that a gourmet spread is wasted on someone who's hungry enough to see anything edible as nothing more than fuel.

At the other end of the scale were the elk tenderloins I brought frozen from home and cooked three days into a trip on the bank of a cutthroat trout stream in Wyoming. I hovered like a mother hen and got them perfectly medium rare on a portable wire grill over an open fire and served them with pork and beans. Quick, simple, and really good. On any fishing trip there can be a time and place for a celebratory meal—and sometimes the time is determined by when the meat will go bad.

It's getting rare in these days of catch-and-release fishing, but in some places the great tradition of the shore lunch still survives. This is when you take a long-enough break at noon to build a fire and grill fish fresh from the water where they were caught, along with canned beans or fried potatoes and, if you want to get fancy, biscuits baked in a Dutch oven. This usually happens in far-flung regions that are so lousy with fish that being able to keep a few for lunch is a foregone conclusion. Closer to home, some fishermen still carry small, light frying pans in their daypacks, and one friend of mine has a dozen wire grills stashed in isolated places he likes to fish, although he usually also carries crackers and a can of sardines for slow days.

Sometimes when I'm out fishing I'll stumble on someone's old lunch spot. There'll be a grown-over fire ring with disintegrating charcoal and, somewhere nearby, a pile of old steel cans that have rusted to what look like rinds of reddish-brown lace. Usually these are in a spot that's shaded by trees and has a nice view of the water. Technically, this amounts to litter, but I've never minded.

I've also had some great food on guided trips where, as the pros say, the weather, the fishing, and the skill of the clients are all up for grabs, but meals are the one thing the guide can control.

There was a certain hot lunch on a river in Oregon that stands out. It was a raw, rainy day in February, with that humid, bone-deep chill you get in the Pacific Northwest. On the first run we fished right at dawn, a seam in my seven-year-old waders suffered a catastrophic failure and I went through the morning with my left leg wet to the crotch. At noon, our guide put my partner and me on a good-looking run, found a spot out of the rain, and grilled a couple of herb-marinated chickens on a hibachi. I was uncomfortably cold, but I think I was still this side of hypothermic, although it's hard to be sure because judgment is among the first things to go. Maybe they were organic, free-range chickens, I don't know, but they were hot and delicious and may have saved my life.

There was a wonderful lunch of pasties out in an open boat on Lake Superior. A pasty sounds like something a stripper would wear, but it's actually a meat, rutabaga, potato, and onion–filled pie common in northern Michigan. They're best when served hot, but even at ambient summer temperatures—and when you're really hungry—they're the blue-collar equivalent of beef Wellington.

I seem to remember a fancy shore lunch on the Eagle River in Colorado that began with paté on thin, fragile crackers, but that one is so vague I can't swear it isn't a product of my imagination. I mean, who do I know who'd serve such a thing?

And there was a chilly morning in camp on the Deschutes River in Oregon when I was up before dawn for a few hours of swinging with a spey rod, during which I watched the sun rise over volcanic cliffs and landed two steelhead. Then I headed back to camp with my stomach growling and walked straight into the unmistakable aromas of bacon, pancakes, and coffee. If you look up "happiness" in a dictionary, you'll see a picture of me sitting down to that breakfast.

14.

LIVIN' THE DREAM

I don't have a GPS in my pickup, but I'd gotten directions to the place where I'd be staying a few miles outside of Bozeman, Montana, from the AAA website. They were on the money for 684 miles—right up until I turned off Highway 85 onto a series of dirt roads, at which point they went terribly wrong. Apparently the computer had been programmed to just make something up rather than admit it didn't know the route—an almost endearingly human trait. Finally a friendly man on a bicycle pointed the way to a massive log house with several obvious fishing-guide vehicles parked outside: large crew-cab pickups with trailer hitches, rod caddies, and tackle company stickers obscuring the view out the back windows. This had to be the place.

I'd been invited there to attend the third annual ICE OUT event, a kind of convention for fishing guides put on free of charge by Simms Fishing Products, which is headquartered in Bozeman. According to Peter Vandergrift, Simms's guide desk manager and the event's organizer, 520-some guides from around the United States and Canada had registered to attend, along with another hundred people from sponsor companies like R. L. Winston Rods and Ro Drift Boats. Bozeman has doubled in size since I first passed through in the 1970s, but even now six-hundred-plus extra fishermen would make a dent, although they wouldn't exactly stand out in a town where trailered drift boats are a common feature of what passes for morning rush hour.

When we talked about this on the phone I asked Peter about the possibility of fishing (already thinking about playing hooky). He allowed that some people did sneak off to wet a line and rattled off a list of nearby rivers—the Yellowstone, Gallatin, Madison, Big Hole, etc.—that sounded like the standard Montana dream-trip itinerary. Then again, ICE OUT was scheduled for early April, when the rivers were just going into runoff and not the best time to fish in the region, but of course, that was the idea. If they held this event at the height of the season, when guides could be out making a living, no one would come.

I think there were seven of us actually staying at the house, but it was hard to be sure as strange faces came and went over the next few days. I met Rod and Arlo and a guy named Ernest, who was from south Texas and the only person I talked to at the event who guided with spinning rods instead of fly tackle. Marty and Brian were steelhead guides I'd fished with in Oregon. They asked about some mutual acquaintances. Robert and his seventeen-year-old golden retriever, Belican, were from southern Colorado, and we also had friends in common. "That's like 'pelican,' only with a *B*," he said helpfully, "after a brand of beer from Belize."

It took only about ten minutes to establish that all these guys either knew or knew *of* each other or had outfitters, rivers, clients, and industry reps in common. To some, guiding is just a summer job that beats flipping burgers in a dopey hat, but those who have gone on to make it a profession form an exclusive community, and even among strangers there's rarely more than one degree of separation.

At one point Peter had referred to this place as the Ambassador House—making it sound like a moderately classy hotel—but what he meant was that everyone staying there except me qualified as what Simms called a "guide ambassador." That would be, he said, a guide with anywhere from "ten to fifty years' experience who helps us promote Simms at the highest level." That sounded a little vague, but I got the idea. In a different kind of business, these would be the guys with Salesman of the Year plaques hanging in their offices.

I'd been offered the option of my own room in town, but the house seemed like the obvious choice. For one thing, it was right on a pretty stretch of the Gallatin River. For another, I didn't want to be one of those correspondents who file their stories from the safety of a hotel bar; I wanted to be embedded with the troops. Someone said this was like the setup for a reality show: six guides, an old dog, and a writer stuck in a house together, only there'd be no prize money for the survivor. Someone else peeked into the refrigerator and was happy to find no food but what looked like about eighty cans of beer, presumably courtesy of Simms.

The event went on for the next three days, and if you wanted to—and some did—you could attend scheduled functions, including cocktail parties, from 8:30 or 9:00 in the morning until way past bedtime. The first morning I had a big breakfast at a place called the

Kountry Korner Cafe and then went on the obligatory Simms factory tour. I was unfamiliar with the process and assumed that modern waders would be stamped out robotically like Toyotas, but in fact the work resembled tailoring and was done mostly by hand, by people the company refers to as "wader artisans." That sounds like corporate hyperbole, but actually this is skilled work that not just anyone off the street could do. Most artisans are trained in several different jobs and are periodically shuffled around to head off repetitive motion injuries: the assembly-line equivalent of black lung.

Afterward I sat outside at a picnic table and watched wader- and raincoat-clad volunteers step into a kind of enclosed mobile shower with fans and clear plastic walls that simulated two or three minutes of monsoon-level downpour. Of course, the real test of waders and rain gear is a week's worth of ten-hour days in a steady drizzle, but it looked like fun, everyone came out dry and smiling, and the point was made.

There were two cocktail parties that day—one at 4:30 ("use your green drink tickets"), the other at 9:00—but very little evidence of public drunkenness. That evening coach Bobby Knight gave a talk called "Perspective from the Front Seat" (where the client sits in a drift boat). He mostly just talked about basketball, but no one seemed to mind. There was also a short-film contest in which participants were given a single day to shoot fishing footage on nearby water and edit it together. The results were predictably mediocre.

The seminar schedule hinted at some of the day-to-day concerns of a working guide: "Marketing Your Guide Business," "My Gear, Water & Tactics," "Planning for a Life in Guiding: Financing, Health, and Guiding Green," "Fishing the World Without Any Money" (that one was standing-room only), "Correcting the Cast," and "Correcting the Two-Handed Cast." (That would be the client's cast, not the guide's.) Other subjects might have included taxes, insurance, liability issues, and marriage counseling, but there was only so much time.

I found some of this informative because I'm morbidly curious about how other people manage to make a living, but I come from the Midwest, where direct questions about health and finance are considered rude, so I can't come right out and ask. It hardly matters anyway, since it always boils down to hard work, clear thinking, thrift, and attention to detail. I do understand the nature of the problem, if not the day-to-day scope. My own life as a writer is sometimes in shambles because the business end isn't the fun part, so I often neglect it until my career is visibly circling the drain.

I didn't last all the way through the "Product Feedback Sessions," where guides frankly tell the company what they think of their products, but what I saw was impressive. A few criticisms were laughably picky, but most seemed perceptive and useful: the kind of thing that could come only from people who use this stuff not so much as sporting equipment but as tools of their livelihood and put hundreds of days of hard wear on their gear in a single season.

At one point there was a discussion of how to properly care for breathable GORE-TEX waders. Wash by hand in a bathtub with cold water and mild detergent, then rinse several times and air-dry inside and out, with an elapsed time of no less than twenty-four hours—more in a damp climate. There was general agreement when a young guide asked, "Who the hell has time for that?"

The guides sat, stood, and sometimes came and went carrying water bottles or cups of coffee. There were maybe seventy-five of them in the room at any one time. Three company people were at the front of the room behind a folding table. One stood and moderated while the others sat and took notes, one on a laptop, the other on a yellow legal pad. They seemed genuinely interested, and although the meeting wasn't overly serious, it still had the no-nonsense air of a NASA debriefing session.

That was typical. When I decided to come to this event I had half expected—and as a writer maybe even hoped for—a Sturgis-style madhouse with a fly-fishing theme. What I found instead were a bunch of career fishing guides intent on perfecting their profession, which is not to say that you'd have mistaken this for a conference of Lutheran ministers. Most of the events seemed well attended, but none of them matched the crowds at the cocktail parties, where people hooted, told stories and jokes, held their hands out to demonstrate the size and shape of fish, exchanged maps drawn on the backs of napkins, and compared scars. The best scar was from a gruesome bout with a flesh-eating virus. The best joke was: "What's the difference between a large pizza and a fishing guide? A large pizza can feed a family."

Twice I snuck out to fish the Gallatin for a few hours with guys from the house on the theory (or the excuse) that hanging out with real-live guides would be more educational than formal events. The first time I didn't bother checking the schedule to see what I was missing. The second time I ended up skipping the "Guide Olympics" at the Montana State University field house, where the events included casting for distance and accuracy, rod rigging against the clock, a beer-filled cooler pull, and competitive trailer backing through an obstacle course. A guide from the Northwest later told me he'd have done better in the trailer competition if the conditions had been more realistic—that is, if it had been held before dawn and in the rain.

There was some talk one evening about the appearance of professionalism. Dave Whitlock said that guides should be polite, soft-spoken, and show up for work clean, well dressed, well groomed, and having used deodorant that morning. I thought about the good guides I've fished with. A few fit that description—fresh haircuts, pressed khakis, calling people "Sir" and "Ma'am"—but many others, including some of the best, were scruffy, wrinkled, and rough around the edges in other ways and could be accurately described as characters, if not outright river rats.

Of course, it *is* best not to frighten or gross out your clients, but I think professionalism and the showmanship that comes with it are harder to pin down. Guiding and being guided is a weirdly intimate affair, with no room for bluffing on either side, but plenty of opportunities for style and creativity. Together you'll experience drama, disappointment, maybe success, and at least a moderate dose of the unexpected under a variety of conditions. This is the kind of thing that reveals character. After a day on the water, your guide may know you better than people you've worked with for years. After a week, he may know more about who you really are than your mother. In extreme cases, a guide's ability to quickly figure out how to joke or cajole you out of anything from run-of-the-mill frustration to despondency can make or break a day on the water.

The good ones combine the generosity of a teacher, the craftiness of a psychiatrist, and the enthusiasm of a cheerleader with a kind of Vulcan detachment, and they make it look easy. A perfect day of guiding is like a perfect piece of writing: you don't see the hair pulling, navel-gazing, bouts of depression, or the dozen discarded drafts, and the part you do see looks effortless. The client thinks, *Hell, I could do that.*

And on top of everything else, a guide also functions as a surrogate fishing buddy. You'll now and then hear people say of a guide they fished with, "I'm sure most of the people he takes out are just clients, but he and I actually got to be friends." Of course it does happen, but in fact the best guides send everyone home thinking the same thing. It's part of the job description. A waiter I know once said, "In my business, it's not important that I like you; it's only important that you *think* I like you." That struck me as either the height of cynicism or the very definition of service.

The final event was the "Super Sale," held in the banquet room of the GranTree Inn. Robert, Belican, and I had lingered on the Gallatin River after his streamside entomology talk, and by the time we got there the place was mobbed. This was the first time I'd have said that all 620-some attendees plus staff were in the same place at the same time.

Virtually everyone had a beer in hand, possibly not their first of the evening. The banquet room was packed with people shouting to be heard over all the other people shouting to be heard, and the temperature inside was pushing a hundred degrees from combined body heat. The deals on seconds and discontinued merchandise were said to be too good to believe, and several of us were standing outside where it was cool, watching the sun set toward the Madison Range and wondering whether we wanted to go in. (I, for one, didn't really need anything.) A guy passed by and said all he wanted was a raincoat for his wife. Half an hour later we were still there when he came back out, lugging a lawn-and-garden–sized trash bag crammed with stuff and looking sheepish. I decided not to go in after all.

The Gallatin had come up, gone off-color, and was no longer really fishable. Two guys said that in the morning they were going over to look at the Big Hole. A few others talked about streamer fishing the Yellowstone. Still others planned to hit more distant rivers on their way home. People kept coming out of the hotel with their arms loaded with gear, but if anything, the racket from inside had gotten louder. There was the sense of something simultaneously gearing up and winding down.

My observations? Guides work hard. No—I mean even harder than you think. My own short stint as a guide years ago doesn't give me any special insight, because I didn't last long enough to get the full picture. I did learn the first lesson—that if your client catches fish, it's because he's the best fisherman in the world, but if he doesn't, it's the guide's fault—but that brief glimpse was enough to make me bolt and get a job driving a garbage truck. My friendship with a handful of guides has given me a wider view, but, typically of the breed, these guys aren't complainers. They're more likely to describe the worst trip of the season as "just another day in the life."

Still, I've come to understand that the effort you see on the water is maybe a third of it, while behind the scenes is the endless maintenance of vehicles, boats, and trailers; daily wrangling of lunches, drinks, and ice for the cooler; arranging for shuttles, phone calls, and e-mails with clients; checking on stream flows, hatches, and weather; and restocking of flies, tippet, floatant, and a bunch of other things you and I wouldn't think of because we don't work as guides but that we'd miss if no one did them.

Even further behind the scenes is the maintenance of professional-looking websites with constantly updated information and high-quality photos and videos, plus Twitter feeds, Facebook updates, and God knows what all else. The guy who, only a generation ago, could have gotten away with being a simpleminded backwoods loner now has to know as much about pixels and gigabytes as he does about Green Drakes. Word of mouth from happy fishermen is still the best advertising a guide can have, but there's now the danger that the jungle telegraph will be drowned out by a barrage of electronic hype.

And that's not to mention keeping the books, paying the taxes, occasional awkward conversations with bankers, lack of sleep, a diet containing too much junk food, the strain of long hours on your homelife . . . in short, all the drudgery and heartbreak of running a small business on a shoestring, now and then exacerbated by clients who clap you on the back and say, "What a life you have. You get paid to do nothin' but fish." To which you can only reply, "Yeah, man, I'm livin' the dream here."

So it's not surprising that some guides affect an air of superiority, and yes, the tales they tell about their clients usually do involve some kind of buffoonery, but that's just the nature of storytelling. The right weather, a perfect stream flow, and a good fisherman with realistic expectations doesn't make much of a story for the same reason you'll never see a newspaper headline that reads, "Things Actually Went Pretty Smoothly Today."

Of course, there *is* that minor subgenre of sportswriting in which professional guides—usually young bloggers—relate their experiences from the vantage point of "We're the pros who know the score, while everyone else is pretty much an idiot." This is the kind of thing you sometimes have to get off your chest after a few seasons of not yelling at clients even when they have it coming and not stepping on their favorite rods even when they put them where they're begging to get stepped on, but in the end it may not be the best career move, since those idiots constitute the majority of your potential readership.

But most guides talk about these things only among themselves—and at a three-day convention attended by hundreds of them, you can get an earful.

One guy told me that most of the problems he had with clients amounted to simple LOFT issues.

"LOFT?" I asked.

"Lack of Fucking Talent."

Interestingly, though, these stories are usually less about ridicule and more about an appreciation for the infinite varieties of human nature, and if there's one thing all successful guides have in common, it's a durable sense of humor. I mean, really, what other profession could give you this many laughs?

15.

OLIVES

When the power went off during an April snowstorm, I plugged the chest freezer into the generator so the food wouldn't spoil. This was the new generator, a 3,600-watt Yamaha that mutters politely in the background, unlike the old Briggs & Stratton I used to have that made such a racket I was tempted to trade my frozen steaks for some peace and quiet. We're on a rural electric co-op here, and the power goes off three or four times a year on average—not always for obvious reasons like weather—so a generator is standard equipment.

We got only two or three inches of snow in the valley before it turned to sleet and then rain, but just to the north, through the rest of Larimer County and on into southern Wyoming, as much as fifty inches of wet snow fell in three days, clinging to power lines like kudzu, and that was all she wrote. You forget that your house is an electric appliance until it abruptly goes dark.

By then we'd been fishing the spring Blue-Winged Olive hatches for three weeks, trying to pick out the gray, rainy days that both the trout and the mayflies like. There's always some urgency to this pre-runoff season, because it can turn sour at a moment's notice as it did in April. The weather was still fine for fishing in a hood-up-on-the-rain-slicker sort of way, but after days of snow and rain the water was high, muddy, and cold, so the hatches would be off for a while. This was still too early for the seasonal melting of the mountain snowpack that swells the rivers with muddy ice water and blows six to eight weeks of fishing, but these shoulder seasons are short enough as it is, and you hate losing days to temporary storm runoff.

It had started beautifully back in late March, when we drove to the South Platte River thinking it might not be too early for Olives. I'd already been out a few times, starting in February at the inlet to a nearby reservoir, where I snaked my casts between chunks of dislodged shelf ice and managed some holdover stocked rainbows. This spot gets crowded later in the season, but that day I had it to myself except for a lone dog walker who gave me a look you'd normally reserve for someone fishing in a bathtub.

I was having an awful time with my knots. I hadn't forgotten how to tie them over the winter, but I was rusty, so my loops went cattywampus, my bitter end had a mind of its own, and my frozen fingers felt like they belonged to a corpse, but those were still my first trout of the new year, so things were looking up.

I got out a few more times after that—and fishing really is like riding a bike—so by the time I went to the South Platte I had my river legs again. I drove down with one friend and met another on the river, and we caravanned miles downstream out of the crowd to a stretch that's not fished as hard. There are no actual secrets on a popular tailwater an hour's drive from Denver, but there *is* water that's overlooked by some fishermen, and you wouldn't mind keeping it that way. So when you're playing a trout here and a car passes on the county road, you're torn between holding the bent rod high to show off and acting like you've accidentally hooked a bush.

The Olives came off around one o'clock, and I found three fish rising in a short glide: two smaller ones in open water and what looked like a bigger one tucked in beside a rock. I tried one of the smaller fish first to see if I'd guessed right on the fly pattern. Blue-Winged Olives are a ubiquitous western hatch that comes off both spring and fall, so like most regional fishermen I carry no fewer than half a dozen different Olive patterns. My go-to is still the old quill-bodied parachute that now seems as dated but dependable as a Rolls-Royce, but if it always worked I wouldn't have to carry the others. One of the smaller fish ate a size-20 parachute on the third or fourth cast, but the little hook didn't bite, and the commotion of the missed strike spooked both fish. At least it was the right fly.

I waded into position for the trout that was still rising next to the rock. He was holding in a four-inch-wide tongue of current that had begun as melting snow in the mountains and was now hurrying toward the main branch of the Platte in Nebraska, then to the Missouri, then the Mississippi, and on to the Gulf of Mexico. Once there some of it would evaporate, join an upslope front, and fall as mountain snow again, endlessly repeating the cycle. This is the same water we've always had—brought by comets billions of years ago, they say—and it's the only water we'll ever have, but for the moment this global system was reduced to the eighteen inches of dead drift I'd need to get that trout to eat my fly—which it did. I didn't have a landing net that day, but managed to beach him gently and release him: a fifteen-inch wild brown, fat for his length and a real specimen. Then I went looking for another one.

No hatch I know of depends more on weather than Blue-Winged Olives. These drab little mayflies like to emerge on cold, gray, wet days, which are coincidentally the same days that make the brown and rainbow trout in these tailwaters more eager to feed at the surface. So clouds are good, drizzle is ideal, and light rain is fine, although an outright downpour will put off the hatch for at least as long as it lasts, and sometimes longer. And Olives don't mind snow, which explains the stories you'll sometimes hear from people who saw a trout stream in a snowstorm and swore the fish were eating the flakes. On the other hand, both the trout and the mayflies cringe at direct sunlight like spelunkers emerging from a cave into a bright afternoon.

That day on the South Platte began with a thick overcast that got the hatch going nicely, but by midafternoon patches of blue began to blow over and sunlight burst onto the river, with predictable results. The hatching flies would immediately thin out, and the rises would sputter and stop in the time it takes to wake up from a dream and realize where you are. When clouds covered the sun again, it wasn't like flipping a switch back on. It could take ten minutes for the bugs to get going, and another ten for the fish to notice and start rising again. When the sky clouded over for the last time in late afternoon, I understood that the hatch wouldn't come back and ran into the rest of the crew as we were all walking back to the trucks. It's hard to describe, but there's a specific feeling of finality when the fishing is done for the day.

We made a few more trips to the South Platte in the next couple of weeks, and although the hatch petered off each time and we caught some fish, it was never as good as on that first afternoon. For one thing, the days we picked turned out to be no more than partly cloudy, so the bugs were sparse and the rises were spotty. For another, the water board kept bumping the flow out of Cheesman Dam, first from 65 cubic feet per second to 120, and then to 160. Any of those are perfectly good flows for dry-fly fishing if they're stable, but trout can go off their feed when river levels rise suddenly. We say they get confused by the changing conditions and need a few days to acclimate. It's as good an explanation as any.

Also, rising water dislodges lots of the gooey green aquatic vegetation fishermen incorrectly call "moss," and when it's thick it can foul your flies on every other cast until you start thinking about all the productive things you could have been doing if you'd stayed home.

After the worst of that April storm, when the power had come back on but the sky was still gray and drizzly, I drove up to the Big Thompson River below Olympus Dam. I hadn't fished the Thompson since the previous fall, and then only out of curiosity. Like several other streams in the region—with my home water on the St. Vrain drainage at the epicenter—the Thompson took a hit in the flood of 2013, the result of a freaky September storm that dropped nineteen inches of rain in four days in a region that gets only twenty inches in a normal year.

The resulting flood was the kind of thousand-year event that rearranges the landscape overnight. It killed nine people, did millions of dollars' worth of property damage, and washed out three state highways, stranding hundreds of us. It also scoured the steep stretches of my home stream down to the bedrock, depositing what had once been an aquatic insect habitat in new floodplains at the mouths of the canyons.

In the middle of it the river ran so thick with silt that it flowed less like water and more like syrup. I found dead brown trout strangled in mud on what was left of Highway 36. My own place was safe on high ground between the North St. Vrain and the Little Thompson, but recognizable parts of some of my neighbors' houses were washing down the river.

Once the water receded and I could get out of the valley, I spent days locating friends. Some had been evacuated and were staying with friends or in church basements; others had hunkered down in places I couldn't get into and they couldn't get out of. Electricity, phone, and Internet had all been out for over a week, and there's never been cell phone reception in the valley, so it wasn't until I got out that I learned FEMA had listed all of us who'd been stuck north of the North Fork as "unaccounted for," which those unfamiliar with the nomenclature of disaster took to mean missing or dead. So when I got a Wi-Fi signal at a coffee shop in a nearby town, I spent hours answering e-mails from friends and family to assure them I was alive. Most seemed happy to hear it.

I walked parts of the once-familiar riverbed in and around the small town of Lyons and wouldn't have known where I was if it weren't for the surviving landmarks. I met a man who said he was looking for unearthed gold nuggets and Indian artifacts and glanced with new interest at the sand at my feet. I met another man who was looking for his Prius. The flood had washed it out of his driveway, but the insurance company wouldn't pay unless he could show them the damaged car, even though they knew full well that it was now buried under tons of sand and gravel, leaking gasoline, motor oil, and battery acid into the water table. (That was the first story I heard about someone being hung out to dry by their insurance company, but it wouldn't be the last.) I said if I found the car, I'd call him. He reminded me that the phones didn't work.

Over the next few weeks a kind of shrine developed in a vacant lot in town as people deposited found items that others might be looking for. Furniture, mailboxes, mismatched silverware, a coatrack, mounted deer antlers, a broken mirror, an empty picture frame, waterlogged family photos. Eventually the town board, in their infinite wisdom, took it all to the dump.

Emotions floated unexpectedly close to the surface. People who were calm, practical, and helpful for days would abruptly snap at nothing, and two weeks in, believing I was used to the new reality, I totally lost it at the sight of a piano wrapped around a cottonwood tree.

When it came to rebuilding, we all did what we could, using tools ranging from shovels to checkbooks. Some also dove down the preposterous rabbit holes of state and federal bureaucracies, only to emerge months later only partly successful and disillusioned by a system that seems stubborn about helping but eager to keep you from helping yourself. During the thick of it people had been anywhere from patient to helpful to heroic as conditions dictated, but as we waded on through the later stages of disaster—which resemble those of grief—a few surprising examples of shittiness emerged. Or maybe not so surprising. As a friend put it, "Those who were assholes after the flood had also been assholes *before* the flood." On the plus side, a Larimer County sheriff's deputy told me, "Ninety-nine percent of you folks have been a pleasure to deal with."

During that first week or so when everyone was still cut off and in need of everything from firewood to food to drinking water to prescriptions to a generator to run a critical medical device, it had been the blue-collar types who had the tools, equipment, knowledge, and levelheadedness to do the heavy lifting. Later, when bumper stickers reading "Lyons Strong" and "We've Got Grit" began to appear, I proposed one that would say "Thank God for the Rednecks," but no one else thought it was a good idea.

Which is to say, it was a long time before I started worrying about the fish.

Over the following winter the Corps of Engineers and the Department of Transportation charged in with heavy equipment and the best intentions and did more damage to the streams than the flood had done. In one spot healthy pine trees were cut from the bank of the stream so the logs could be used in "bank stabilization structures," never mind that the root systems of live trees are better bank stabilization structures than anything you can build. And on the St. Vrain a Parks and Wildlife survey showed that the fish population had gone from 2,004 trout per mile before the flood to 798 after and then to *nine* trout per mile once the DOT and the Corps were finished with it.

I'd fished the Thompson once in October of the following year, when the road reopened thirteen months after the flood. I drove to the river on a day that was threatening snow and found parts of it looking like a cross between a gravel quarry and a landfill. A sparse Olive hatch petered off and I found a few rising trout, two of them in a run with a carpet spread out on the bottom of the pool and the remains of someone's back porch piled up on the far bank. I did make a few casts, but my heart wasn't in it.

When I went back this last time, six months later, the spring Olive hatch was a little heavier than it had been the previous fall—though still stingy by preflood standards—and there seemed to be a few more trout. Still, the fishing would have been disappointing if not for the apparent miracle of these few fish and the weightless little insects they were rising to surviving a flood that washed away a two-lane highway.

The hatch went off around four, and I thought about spending the rest of the day driving downstream to the little town of Drake and then up the North Fork to Glen Haven—both of which had been largely destroyed in the flood—but then decided against it. Disaster tourists usually come from somewhere else. When it all happened in your own backyard, you've already seen enough.

It started raining again in early May; another big storm predicted to bring a week's worth of snow to the higher elevations and hard rain lower down. They'd kept bumping up the flow on the South Platte in sudden, unpredictable increments until it was finally unfishable, so four of us met up on the west slope between Aspen and Basalt. We rented a log house that was built in the 1880s as a stagecoach stop and had since been gussied up for tourists with a microwave and so many throw pillows there was hardly room to sit. This was a cozy place to eat, sleep, and kill our aimless time off the water. For instance, one night after supper one of the guys showed off a new app on his smartphone that would supposedly identify any music you played into it, and some smart-ass stumped it on the first try with an old Lightnin' Hopkins tune. That kind of thing.

Three of the four of us had been in the flood, but it's no longer a topic of conversation except as a time reference. It's not that we're all that stoic; it's just that the well-meaning sympathy we got finally became embarrassing enough that when someone asked, "Were you in that flood?" we'd answer, "Aw, not really," and change the subject. For that matter, after eighteen months we'd long since talked it to death among ourselves, including the part where we'd now have to travel farther from home to fish for the foreseeable future.

The day before I met the others at the cabin, the Colorado River upstream from Dotsero had gone from 950 cubic feet per second the afternoon before to 1,700 the next morning from rain and snow in the headwaters. I floated it with a friend anyway, since we were already there. Size-16 brown caddis flies were hatching in clouds and some Olives were floating around in the backwaters, but the river was the color and clarity of wet cardboard, so the trout couldn't see them.

The Roaring Fork behind our rented cabin was in a little better shape, and we squeezed out a few trout on nymphs, but it was getting muddy, coming up fast, and wouldn't last another day. It was getting harder to believe that this high water was just a temporary setback instead of the beginning of a big spring runoff that would end the early-season reprieve.

But the nearby Fryingpan River is a tailwater, so from the bottom-draw dam down to where Seven Castles Creek poured in brick-red, it was still low and clear, and we were happy to see it. At times like these I agree with my late friend Gary LaFontaine, who said that as a conservationist, he'd fight new dams on free-flowing rivers, but as a fisherman, he'd fish below them when they were inevitably built anyway.

The weather that week couldn't have been better for the Olive hatch. It rained every day, but seldom hard enough to put down the hatch for more than a few minutes at a time. The ceiling of clouds was so low that you felt like you were standing in the sky, and the snow line reached halfway down the canyon, while along the river the dripping cottonwoods, dogwoods, and willows were leafing out and seemed to have gotten thicker and greener every time I looked up from the water. Now and then a hummingbird would buzz incongruously past in weather cold enough to see your breath. At odd moments you might wonder whether this was miserable enough to make you walk back to the truck and run the heater, but then you'd promptly forget about it.

The hatch came off between late morning and early afternoon each day and lasted for hours, with enough bugs on the water to get the trout feeding well, but few enough that they'd still pick your fly out of the crowd. For once it was like the fishing you imagine on the drive to the river but rarely find when you get there. (When you describe to a non-angler the kind of ideal conditions you're always hoping for, they'll ask, "Jeez, when do you ever get out?")

Most of the trout we caught were the ten-inch browns that our friend Will at the fly shop in town says are overpopulating the river and should be thinned out, but there were enough bigger rainbows to keep you on your toes: sixteen to eighteen inches long, and one just over twenty-one inches—as measured against my landing net—that ate a size-20 Olive and tail-walked across the river, with its wide red stripe far and away the brightest thing in the landscape. Later one of my friends said, "That must have been a big trout, because you're not usually one to whoop when you hook up."

"Did I whoop?" I asked.

It was still raining when I got home from the Pan, and the North and South Forks of the St. Vrain were brown and foamy and out of their banks, although that's not the benchmark it once was, because the river had rearranged the landscape, so the banks are no longer where they used to be. This turned out to not be as dire as it looked, but we were all a little skittish now, so sheriff's deputies were stationed at the bridges for a few nights to keep an eye on the river, just in case.

I went down to look at the river myself and stood there wondering how I could so dearly love something that's really just an example of water obeying the laws of physics. But a river running too high and muddy to catch trout on dry flies isn't the worst that can happen, and, like everyone else I know, I had plenty of things to do besides go fishing; I just couldn't think of any of them at the moment.

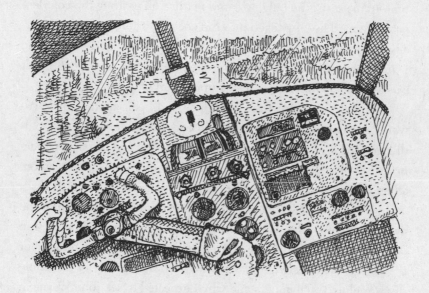

16.

FLOATPLANES

My first flight in a floatplane was in northern Canada sometime in the late 1970s. I don't remember the exact year, but I remember the plane. It was a de Havilland Twin Otter: a big workhorse of an aircraft that carried ten fishermen, all our gear, a week's worth of groceries and supplies, and a fifty-five-gallon drum of gas a hundred-some miles north to a lodge in the Northwest Territories. Flying in a floatplane had been a boyhood fantasy, so I tried to soak it all up: the aluminum ladder leading to the rounded hatch, the unforgiving tube-frame seats, the bulging cargo netting, all wearing the colorless patina of hard use. I peeked into the cockpit, where a pilot in coveralls was fiddling with mysterious knobs and hydraulic levers as the twin engines warmed up. I had no idea what I was looking at, but it was unbearably romantic in a steampunk sort of way.

The flight up there from Winnipeg had been another first. We were in a Douglas DC-3, the sausage-shaped, twin-engine tail-dragger you'll recognize from old newsreel footage of paratroopers in World War Two and of the early days of commercial aviation, when flying was such a special occasion that women wore dresses and white gloves and men sported coats and ties. I peeked into the cockpit here, too (this was back in the days when you could peek into cockpits without getting arrested). If you're old enough to remember the 1954 movie *The High and the Mighty*, the mother of all airline disaster films, you'll understand why I expected to see John Wayne at the controls.

That old plane triggered the sense I still have that by flying into the far north I was traveling back in time to when people were industrious, uncomplicated, and self-reliant, and fish were fat, plentiful, and innocent. I'd become a writer by then, but hadn't yet learned that the job was one of observation rather than an opportunity to grandstand, so I kept thinking things like, "Our hero strides aboard this ancient airplane without a thought for his own safety," whereas in fact I was hoping this tin can could still get airborne. I mean, really, a car that old would have been in a museum.

That was a good trip. We caught big mackinaws and pike in the lake and fat grayling in the river, and I released what at the time would have been the world-record fly-caught lake whitefish without so much as a snapshot for proof. I also saw my first wolves. They seemed less like majestic symbols of wildness and more like stray dogs as they picked through the camp garbage, but they were, by God, genuine timber wolves!

I didn't see any caribou, but so many of them migrated through there in the off-season—shedding their antlers as they went—that a normal spring chore was to collect the sheds and toss them on a pile in the middle of camp that by then had grown to a height of ten feet and looked like some kind of mute Stone Age monument.

Another spring chore was to straighten up a couple of graves on a rise overlooking the lake, resetting the sandblasted wooden crosses and crude board fences. These graves were maintained out of a free-floating sense of decency, even though no one knew for sure how old they were or who was buried there. Some claimed it was old French explorers; others said it was just a couple of trappers, and one of the guides elbowed me in the ribs and said they were unruly clients from last season. This was the kind of place you could reach only by float-plane.

A few years later, on a trip to Alaska, I flew in my first Beaver. A succession of three of them, actually, as a couple of us bounced from lodge to lodge on the kind of frenetic junket only a tourist bureau could dream up. Their conditions ranged from a fully refurbished purple number with white lightning bolts freshly painted down each side to a faded yellow one that was sound as a dollar mechanically but as dingy and threadbare inside as an old school bus. I'd never seen one of these in the flesh before, but they looked familiar from a childhood of leafing through dog-eared copies of *Field & Stream* and dreaming of fishing not with my uncle on a tame bass pond but with a bush pilot in trackless backcountry where I'd do battle with enormous, violent fish.

It turned out that a de Havilland DHC-2 Beaver with its beefy fuselage, 48-foot wingspan, and 982-cubic-inch Pratt & Whitney radial engine was several times more impressive in person than in photos. The planes were bigger than I expected, and the literally deafening roar of those engines said these aircraft meant business. After even a short flight my ears would continue to buzz for a while, and all sounds,

151

from human voices to birdsong, seemed to be coming from underwater. The first time this happened there was a pleasant association that I couldn't identify. Then I placed it as the same jittery excitement—half physical, half emotional—that I once felt when walking out onto a quiet city street with my ears ringing after a rock concert. I've since learned to wear foam earplugs on small planes to avoid permanently damaging my hearing.

There are lighter, faster, and sometimes even quieter floatplanes than Beavers, but as E. Donnall Thomas Jr. once wrote, something like a PA-18 Super Cub "couldn't carry much more than one friend, our fly rods, and survival gear—fine for a fly-out day trip, but utterly inadequate to set up a two-week float." I've been on Beavers that easily hauled a pilot, a guide, four fishermen, camping and fishing gear, a week's worth of food, a small generator, gas cans, canoe paddles, and an outboard motor with room left over. A Beaver is the three-quarter-ton crew-cab pickup with a towing package to the Super Cub's Audi sedan.

It's not so much that Beavers make good bush planes as that they were specifically designed and *built* to be bush planes. They can get airborne in a gut-wrenchingly short space using sheer brute force and, according to factory specs, can carry a payload of up to 2,100 pounds. These planes are sexy-looking in the boxy, plainspoken way of a Conestoga wagon, which is to say their glamour derives entirely from where they can take you. That would be into roadless backcountry where the place-names may not be all that exotic but where you might be fishing with the person who named them. I once caught some beautiful brook trout from Victoria Creek in Labrador, and given Canada's history with England, I asked if it was named after the former queen. My guide said, "No, I named it after my daughter—because they're both pretty little things."

We got to Victoria Creek in a Beaver operated by a flying service in Quebec called Air Saguenay. This was a striking fire-engine-red plane with a white tail suggesting spread wings and a racing stripe that resolved into the neck and head of a goose—the company's logo. It was piloted by a French-Canadian named Pierre. He spoke no English and we spoke no French, so he just grinned and pantomimed the plane's salient safety features in the order that you might need them: seat belts, fire extinguisher, first-aid kit, doors.

Pierre lived in a tent. I don't mean that he sometimes *stayed* in a tent, he *lived* in one: a small canvas wall tent with a sheepherder's stove for heat that he preferred over a bunk in the guides' shack at camp, a room in town, or even his mother's house, where he pitched the tent in the backyard over the winter, coming inside for showers and meals at the kitchen table. In all other ways he seemed perfectly normal.

One late afternoon as we broke down our gear after fishing, Pierre chunked up three of the Arctic char we'd killed, put them in a plastic tub with olive oil, lime juice, garlic, and chopped onion, and slipped them under one of the backseats, where the natural motion of the plane would keep the mixture agitated on the flight back from the river. In camp we ate this wonderful ceviche with saltine crackers, and since talking was pointless, we grinned and nodded as if we each thought the others were simpleminded. Leave it to a Frenchman to surmount a language barrier with good food—not to mention having olive oil and garlic within arm's reach at all times.

I've also flown a few times on single-engine Otters. The de Havilland Otter is a later, larger version of the Beaver, with a longer wingspan, more horsepower, and a capacity of ten passengers—conceived as, and originally *known* as, the King Beaver. This is usually the plane that flies you into camp and that you don't see again until it's time to fly back out a week later, but I was at one high-occupancy lodge in the Canadian Arctic that had its own Otter on-site to rotate larger groups out to more remote camps.

The pilot told me that the previous year one of the fishermen had said he'd flown a similar Otter as a spotter in Vietnam—it had been equipped with wheels instead of pontoons then—and when they checked the ID numbers, the guy said that this was, in fact, the very same aircraft. It was a coincidence, but not an unbelievable one, since many of these planes have been passed from hand to hand for over half a century and can turn up anywhere. The pilot said the guy got sort of emotional. In a quavering voice he said, "I almost died in this plane," but didn't volunteer any details. Then he asked if he could fly it, just for old times' sake, although of course, the camp's liability insurance prohibited that.

But then the pilot added that he *did* let the guy sit up front, and I'd noticed for myself that the plane was equipped with dual controls. I got the distinct impression that if this sentimental vet had taken the yoke for a few minutes on a fly-out, the insurance company would never have known about it.

Fine for him, but as much as I love flying in floatplanes, I've never had the slightest hankering to operate one. Just being a passenger makes me feel plenty intrepid enough, and frankly, I'm not the kind of meticulous, technical guy who'd be good at it. Once a friendly pilot explained to me what all the controls in a Beaver did using language he wouldn't have considered particularly technical. Afterward I nodded and asked, "But which one makes it go up?"

I did once briefly take the stick, though. We were flying out of a lodge in Alaska in a Beaver with dual controls, and I was sitting up front enjoying the view, trying not to touch anything, and thinking how much the instrument panel of this plane resembled the dashboard of a 1946 Plymouth. But the pilot, who was also a photographer, thought it would be a hoot to get a photo of me supposedly flying the plane, so he told me to take the yoke and hold it level while he shot frame after frame of me through a wide-angle lens. I never saw the photos, but I'm told they didn't turn out. I was trying to act nonchalant, but I must have looked like I was facing a firing squad.

The first Beavers were made in 1947, and they went out of production a scant twenty years later in 1967. They're so ubiquitous in the far north that it's hard to believe that less than 2,000 were ever built—exactly 1,657, according to one source. There have been casualties over the years, but these things were built to last, and many are still in service somewhere in the world. You see them all over the place in Canada and Alaska, and some have been repaired, rebuilt, and upgraded so many times you wonder how much of the original aircraft remains. I was born in 1946, so I'll never have the pleasure of flying in a Beaver that's older than I am. The oldest one I've knowingly been in was built in 1952. That would have made it sixty years old at the time I was chauffeured around Kodiak Island in it in 2012, and it purred like a kitten, while virtually everything else produced in 1952 is now moldering in a landfill.

No one seems to know how many Beavers are still in use—"hundreds" is the best guess anyone is willing to make—but even with a limited and dwindling supply they're everyone's first choice for a floatplane, and a clean, low-hour Beaver can cost in the neighborhood of half a million dollars. A not-so-clean Beaver will run you less, but it can cost well into six figures to make it airworthy, not counting the staggering ongoing expenses of fuel, maintenance, and insurance. All of which means that many of those who love Beavers the most because they fly them every day can't afford to own one: another item on life's long list of injustices.

On the other hand, a pilot once told me that after a summer of flying sports in and out of remote fish camps he actually looked forward to the off-season when he could move back to town, with restaurants, movies, hot showers, clean sheets, and his long-suffering wife to cuddle with. He said he didn't miss flying one little bit, but the assumption is that being a bush pilot is a calling as well as a job, and I couldn't help but wonder if there were days when this guy would hear the drone of a single-engine prop plane and feel like an albatross with a broken wing. But maybe that's just my tendency to shoehorn everything into the nearest available cliché. To me, climbing aboard a floatplane is either the beginning or the end of an adventure, but maybe to the pilot it's just another day at work.

We now take it so much for granted that we forget what a recent development flying is. My maternal grandmother was born in 1881, only three generations ago, and twenty-two years before the Wright Brothers' first flight. When she died in 1961, she'd managed to live her entire eighty years without ever getting on an airplane. Why? Because, she said, "If the Good Lord had intended for us to fly, He'd have given us wings." When she traveled—which wasn't often—she went by train. Apparently the Good Lord *did* intend for us to hurtle through the landscape at sixty miles an hour while sitting in a chair.

I don't think she missed much, and she probably wouldn't have gotten past security. (Grandma was the kind of dignified old lady who wouldn't have stood still for being patted down by a stranger.) Flying in a commercial jet at thirty thousand feet isn't especially fun, because you're too high to see much beyond the geometric shapes of tilled fields, the smoggy sprawl of cities, or a wilderness of clouds; all amazing sights in their own right, but not what you'd call riveting. The view is so uninteresting that I try to get an aisle seat so I can stretch at least one leg and get to the bathroom without crawling over two other people. The best you can hope for from commercial flying is that the trip will be uneventful and they won't lose your luggage.

But flying in a floatplane is flying the way it should be. You might be going a hundred miles an hour a hundred feet off the ground: low enough and slow enough to identify wildlife on the order of caribou, bears, moose, musk oxen, wolves, and even trumpeter swans. It's a bird's-eye rather than a god-like view. You'll see rocky glacial eskers under the surface of lakes and think about the lake trout that are probably collected around them, and gaze strategically at the pools and riffles of feeder creeks. Every time I've seen pods of salmon in a river from the air, I've thought of the passage in Hemingway's *The Old Man and the Sea* where Santiago thinks he'd like to ride in an airplane so he could fly over the ocean and look down at the fish.

Of course, as a responsible adult I now have the required misgivings about the obscene amounts of fossil fuel floatplanes burn, the air and noise pollution they produce in otherwise clean, silent places, the oil slicks they sometimes leave behind, and the knowledge that the second I land on a pristine lake or river, it becomes that much less pristine because of my presence. But even knowing now that it can never be entirely unambiguous, I always get the same rush when I walk down to a floatplane tied up at a dock, riding high on its pontoons and bobbing gently in the chop: this is the plane that will take me into the kind of wilderness where there's too much water to go anywhere by land and too much land to get very far in a boat.

The way we use it now, "wilderness" is a word that has more to do with emotion than with a specific definition. Saying "wilderness" is like saying "great singer," which could mean anyone from Luciano Pavarotti to Johnny Cash. But one thing it can mean is a region that's still so vast, wet, roadless, and remote that you need a floatplane to get around in it. We go into places like that to catch wild fish, and for more personal reasons that may be complicated or as simple as the urge to escape the present—which admittedly looks none too promising—into, if not the actual past, then at least the kind of timelessness where life still makes sense.

17.

HOME COURT

I never know what to say when I'm asked if one of the places I fish is as good as it was in the old days. Maybe I have a mental picture of pools with big wild trout stacked so thick I can't see the bottom, but what is that, really? A single pool on a single, exceptional day in the 1980s, or three or four decades' worth of accumulated recollections superimposed? For that matter, as far back as I can recall, there were codgers around who claimed that this same river or lake was only a shadow of what it used to be, while we younger guys had begun to suspect that things never really *were* the way they used to be.

The short answer is some places are better, some are worse, and others are about the same, but the biggest difference in most fisheries is that where the old-timers once told stories about trappers, floozies, and bootleggers, their replacements now reminisce about seeing Jimi Hendrix in concert.

I do clearly remember that fly-fishing was intimidating at first—an arcane business that looked like equal parts science and poetry—and all I hoped for on the technical side was simple competence. That seemed unattainable the first time I tried to cast a fly rod, but, lo and behold, simple competence is what I achieved. Now a guide I'm with might tell me it's nice to have a decent fisherman in the boat for a change, but even if he's trolling for a big tip, he won't say I'm the best he's ever seen.

Of course, any definition of "good fisherman" has to include the ability to actually catch fish. I still sometimes have to remind myself of that, since my first fly-fishing was done in the depths of the counterculture of the late 1960s, when some of us thought trout fishing was our ticket to enlightenment. That was a stretch even for a bunch of hippies, but we were young and impressionable, and there *was* that quote from Japanese literature about not lecturing woodcutters and fishermen about Zen because they already knew the score.

Anyway, I read the books and magazines (all of which promised me more and bigger fish) and talked to other fishermen (some of whom were more helpful than others), but what taught me to fish were the lakes, rivers, and streams near home, where I spent entire seasons with no pressure. I was in my twenties, on my own, and could spend my time however I saw fit. After seeing to the necessities of food, rent, and gas money, I saw fit to spend that time trying to catch trout. I thought I was onto something. My father thought I lacked ambition. Neither of us was entirely wrong.

Since then I've grown up and become a productive, tax-paying member of society. I've also traveled farther and caught more and bigger fish, although by temperament I'm still one of those anglers Thomas McGuane once described as "searching less for recreation than for a kind of stillness." On the other hand, I do love to catch fish, and it's on those waters where I have the home-court advantage that I'm most likely to do that.

One chilly day last spring, I was fishing a favorite trout lake with crawdad flies and doing pretty well. I'd been working my way up the east shore, and in the space of half an hour had landed five good-sized trout. That hadn't escaped a couple of guys nearby, who were fishing from belly boats and not getting any takes. Fishermen on the water are always aware of how others are doing, even though we make a show of seeming not to notice. There are those who try to overcome that by yelling, "Fish on!" to no one in particular, but as a native midwesterner I'm too shy to call attention to myself that brazenly. Instead I use loud click and pawl reels that scream like sirens when a fish takes line.

Finally one of these guys kicked his way over and asked, "Okay, what are you doing?" I showed him my rig: a nine-foot rod, a line with a fifteen-foot sink-tip, four feet of eight-pound leader, and a large weighted fly. Then I demonstrated the retrieve. First there's the wait for the sink-tip and fly to settle on the bottom, then the dead-slow hand-twist crawl, punctuated now and then with short strips. I explained that the take could be anything from a hard slam to a slow pull to a tap to a rubbery hesitation that feels like you're hung up on a weed. "Set on anything," I said. I was trying my best to be generous. I was also enjoying being the fisherman who's doing so well a stranger asks him for advice. That doesn't happen every day.

I'd worked out the crawdad business on this lake in fits and starts after I realized the place was lousy with these little freshwater lobsters. I'd find where raccoons had caught and eaten them, leaving piles of shells on the muddy bank along with their own eerily human-looking paw prints. Then I started spotting them in the water, squirting away from my boots when I was wading the shallows. Then a local guide said he thought it must be the crawdads that accounted for the large size of some of the trout here.

I fooled around with existing crawdad patterns until I convinced myself I could do better. First I readjusted my pattern along the lines of a Clouser Minnow so it rode with the hook inverted, making it more likely to hook fish and less likely to foul on the bottom. Then it occurred to me that trout probably weren't seeing crawdads in all the painstaking detail some tiers tried to reproduce. In fact, these crustaceans are so well camouflaged the trout probably weren't seeing them at all unless they moved. And when they did move, that's *all* the fish were seeing: just motion and a vague impression of size.

With that in mind I gradually reduced my once-elaborate crawdad pattern to nothing but rabbit fur palmered onto the hook, along with heavy dumbbell eyes to sink it. I used brownish-gray fur that was as close as I could come to the color of the mud bottom of this lake, and it occurred to me only much later how weird it was to be designing a fly so that the fish *couldn't* see it. The resulting pattern was unattractive by conventional standards—a friend described it as "a fly only its inventor could love"—and so awkward to cast that I ended up naming it the Blunt Force Trauma, but it was quick and painless to tie, thoughtlessly expendable, and the trout liked it better than anything else I'd ever tried.

I arrived at the retrieve by imagining the day-to-day life of a crawdad creeping stiffly along the bottom on its bony legs, hoping not to be noticed by a big, hungry trout but inadvertently giving itself away. I added the occasional abrupt scoot, because that's what they do when they're startled. I thought that sudden motion was something a trout might notice from farther away and maybe come to investigate. Judging from the timing of some strikes, a few of them did.

Being able to picture this seemed important. It gave me faith in what I was doing and kept my mind from wandering to my dwindling bank account and the blinking light on my answering machine. (It's in that distracted moment that I'll sleepwalk through the first strike I've gotten in fifteen minutes.) Groping around on the bottom with an unseen fly lacks the visual pizzazz that first attracted me to fly-fishing, so it's nothing more than purity of intent that allows me to occasionally set the hook on the barest intuition of a take and feel the sudden live weight of a trout on the line. If I can perceive this level of subtlety in the natural world, why can't I figure out the stock market?

It turned out that the same slow-motion retrieve worked for just about everything on this rich, spring-fed lake; possibly because the trout are too well fed and lazy to feel they have to chase anything. There's plenty of violence here (every transaction is a matter of life and death), but the pace is more like that of dairy cows grazing in a pasture. So the trick with sunken flies is a hand-twist retrieve so glacial that someone standing right next to you might ask, "Are you just lettin' it sit out there?"

Some people who fish here will do just that with a brace of nymphs dangled under a strike indicator, letting natural wind drift provide all the movement that's necessary. I've tried that, and it works—especially on slow days when nothing much seems to be going on—but I can't stay with it for long. It's possible that I'd had enough of staring at bobbers by the time I was twelve.

The trout here have earned a reputation for being selective about fly patterns, but the regulars fish an odd assortment of favorite flies that all work in the right hands, although never quite all the time. I try to keep things simple. When trout are eating mayfly duns off the surface, I like a sparsely tied Hare's Ear Parachute, although when a hatch of pale olive Callibaetis mayflies is on I'll often use the Olive Quill Parachute my friend A. K. Best invented back in the late '80s. He and I have had a long-running, half-serious argument over how much difference realistic color makes when imitating specific insects—he says a lot; I say not that much—but this fly is so effective

163

that A.K. feels it wins the argument for him. I refuse to concede the point, but I *have* tied and fished the pattern for over twenty years.

But as a rule, the trout here like nymphs better than dry flies, at least up till the inevitable ten or fifteen minutes at the end of every hatch when there are still a few winged adults floating on the surface but no more emerging nymphs or pupae in the water. Maybe that's because so many fishermen tied on a dry fly the moment they saw a winged insect that over time they trained these fish to be wary of floating patterns. The intelligence of trout is overrated, but once they've been caught and released often enough, it must start to dawn on them that their once-carefree lives are now plagued by booby traps. Even when you end up hooking a confidently feeding trout, you can't shake the feeling that he wasn't entirely fooled by your fly. You'll see the fish slow down, rise cautiously, hesitate, and then nail the fly as if he were trying to snatch something out of a fire without getting burned.

You arrive at this lake by driving slowly up a hill on a rutted two-track road that looks like it could have been made by covered wagons, and your first view of it is cinematic. You top the rise and there it is, puddled in the bottom of a shallow foothills valley with open, grassy banks, a thin stand of willows on the west side and one large, lone cottonwood that shades the universal lunch spot. On windless mornings you can make out the rings of rising trout from four hundred yards.

I can't say why I became so fond of this lake or have been back so often while in the same years I've fished it I've let other new places become pleasant but vague memories. Maybe it's because I can drive there in a little over half an hour, or because it can be so generous one day and so stingy the next. More likely it's because it's located at a low elevation, so you can fish it early and late in the year when the higher mountain lakes are iced up. I can't remember what I thought when I first saw it, but it quickly got under my skin, which is my only explanation for how this kind of thing happens. I once lived for over two decades within sight of a small river that was nothing special, but it regularly lured me away from my livelihood for hours at a time. It didn't help that I have poor work habits and could see the water from my office window.

I do remember that when I first fished this lake, I was no longer a kid at loose ends eager to learn but a fisherman in middle age, with the usual complicated life; still eager enough to learn, but calmer by then, and with a more or less complete skill set. Where I was once the crazy nephew relatives wondered and worried about, I'd finally settled into the role of the Fisherman in the Family, which among non-anglers is affectionate code for "simpleminded but harmless." I knew this had happened when someone stumped for a gift bought me a necktie that looked like a fish. Never mind that I wear ties only to funerals, the one occasion where no one but a fool would wear a tie that looks like a fish.

It took me dozens of return trips to work out the precise shape of the bottom, the location of snags, springs, and weed beds, the seasonal progression of hatches, and some inkling of the logic the fish use to turn all that to their advantage. Not to mention more granular details such as how to get around the spring seeps without sinking into black muck that smells like goose crap and won't rinse off. There are more similarities than differences among trout waters, and I had experience to draw on, but even if you've seen it all before, every body of water has its idiosyncrasies. Learning them takes time and attentiveness, but finally leads to the rare and useful sense of knowing where you are and what you're doing.

The lake is shaped like an irregular, shallow bowl, tipped slightly, with the deep end facing north down the valley. I'm not good at guessing surface acreage, but it isn't large. You could walk around it easily in twenty-five minutes, although I've never made the complete circuit without stopping to cast. The springs that feed it dribble in along the west shore, culminating in the big spring in the southwest corner that gushes so strongly that it has created an alluvial fan of hard sand where you can wade out to cast, although not quite far enough to keep your fly out of the big, loopy willow that stands right where your back-cast has to go.

This spot affords the best view of the valley. There's an expanse of round-shouldered hills and hogbacks to the north, and to the east a ridge of tawny sandstone rimrock capping a boulder-strewn slope that's green, gold, or brown according to the season and either velvety or bristly looking depending on the light. Deer and elk sometimes graze there, and coyotes hunt rabbits among the rocks. I've never seen one, but I've heard them in the evenings. Trout often live in beautiful places, and if you feel like stopping to look, you should. It's not like you're wasting time. And anyway, soon enough you'll be back to scanning the surface of the lake the way a general surveys a battlefield.

Some days this spring hole is the center of the action. Many of the midge hatches are at their thickest here, gradually petering out along the shallow, muddy flats off the south shore, where trout feeding close in are easy to spook, and the ones feeding farther out are hard to reach. That includes the elusive Big Midge, a whopping size-14 maroon-colored chironomid pupa the trout are especially fond of. The Callibaetis mayfly hatch stretches from the spring hole down the weedy west shore, where hooked fish will dive into the vegetation and either break you off or come to the net dragging half a pound of salad.

On sultry summer afternoons the biggest trout in the lake will ease in here to lie with their faces in the cool current from the springs. They're not actively feeding, but a perfectly placed weighted nymph can sometimes tempt them. I've noddled a few exceptionally large rainbows out of here, but I've always felt guilty about it, as if I'd mugged an old lady who was just sitting peacefully in front of her fan on a hot day.

In mid to late May the damselfly nymphs begin to migrate to shore, where they'll crawl up on the weeds to hatch into winged adults. These nymphs are the color of a cooked green bean and smaller than most, and the trout key so specifically on size that a number-16 fly on a 3x long hook is about right, but a slightly larger size-14 can be too big. When they're coming off well it's easy to crouch in the shallows and watch them. They tuck their legs along their sides and wiggle furiously and inefficiently from side to side without making much forward headway, turning themselves into obvious targets. All that effort must tire them out, because now and then they'll stop to rest, splaying their legs out to the side and sinking ever so slowly. I fish the usual slow retrieve with periodic rests while I count to ten as the fly sinks, waiting for the leader to go slack on the surface and then slowly tighten as a cruising trout picks up the fly without leaving so much as a ripple on the surface.

By early June of most years the adult damselflies have hatched and begun their mating swarms. The females are pale olive with clear wings. On sunny days the males look like "iridescent blue needles," just like novelist Craig Nova said. By the time you start flushing these flies out of the tall grass on shore, at least some fish have begun to recognize them as good to eat but hard to catch.

The best tactic is to gently place the fly at the precise point ahead of a cruising fish that's not so close that he'll spook, but not so far away that he'll have too much time to think it over. Exactly how close that is depends on how fast the fish is swimming and its mood, which you tell yourself you can determine from the fish's body language. That guy out there looks bored, but this big boy cruising in from the left is clearly on the prowl. You're trying to create a false first impression that makes the fish lunge and eat the fly on instinct in the same instant it lands on the water.

This takes time, patience, some intuition, good eyes, accurate casting, and a tender hook set, since strikes can be violent enough to snap off the fly. Cruising trout are easier to spot in bright light and glassy water, but they're also more skittish. Cloudy light and a little chop will cover your cast nicely, but can make the fish all but invisible. Every advantage has a corresponding disadvantage, and there are few prolonged flawless performances in fishing, but a handful of trout caught in the same careful way are enough. They make up for a whole day's worth of blown casts and flushed fish, and maybe even for a lifetime spent chasing trout. After all, that's why we fish: for those days when it goes right and you think, *This is all I could have hoped for.*

18.

A BAD DAY

I first fished here during the Ford administration—barely a decade after the dam that turned this from a freestone river into a tailwater was completed—and the three friends I was fishing with date back about as far. We all remember how the hatches have changed as the river continues to settle into its new life as an artificial spring creek (a process a biologist once told me can take over a century). We also think we remember that the trout here used to be bigger, even though our obsolete color slides don't necessarily bear that out. But familiar as it is, this falls short of being our home water. We're veterans in the sense that we've fished the river for going on forty years, but we've maintained our amateur standing by doing it only once or twice a year.

The four of us fell together haphazardly, the way people do, and became friends through the usual mix of proximity, shared interests (including this river), and an ability to put up with one another. By now we all have our assigned roles: there's the guy who compulsively checks texts and e-mails on a variety of electronic devices, the guy who can fix anything and has the tools to do it, the laconic comedian and dispenser of wisdom, and the guy who mercilessly ridicules the first guy for being so busy he has to check his e-mails all the time, which some will recognize as the male equivalent of sympathy.

We've traveled and fished together in various combinations for years, and in that time we've given, taken, and rejected advice, commiserated, argued, helped each other out, and occasionally even risked working together. Nothing threatens a friendship like projects that go south or checks that don't seem big enough, but so far there have been no hard feelings. (On the other hand, one of us claims that his personal motto is "Have no partners.") There have been some changes—some harder to swallow than others—but the biggest one is that when there are this many of us, it can now be harder than it once was to put a trip together. All kinds of things we didn't used to worry about now intrude, like meetings, deadlines, hip replacements, divorces, and the ongoing struggle to make a living that we naïvely thought might get easier as we got older. We bend over backward so that everyone who wants to go can, but at one time or another we've all been casualties of adulthood, grimly taking care of business while our friends went fishing without us.

In other words, we're a typical quartet of fly-fishers who fall somewhere short of elderly but are well past young: the kind of middle-aged dudes who saunter into destination fly shops every day in season with the air of having just gotten the band back together.

We come here because we have the kind of luck I attribute to stubbornness. This river is like a favorite author who could write a book about knitting and we'd still read it, so we'll fish here even when the word from the guys at the fly shop is to leave it alone and try a nearby river known in local shorthand as the Fork.

The advice from the new generation of fly shop guys is better than it was back when people weren't above holding onto the A-list stuff for themselves. Guides then were mostly young folks marking time until they decided what to do with their lives. They ended up on rivers because they loved fishing, and on their rare days off they'd head out early with rods and waders, but you never saw them in the places where they took their clients. Guides today don't love fishing any less, but the profession has begun to look like an entry-level job in the fly-fishing industry, so even the once-secret honey holes are now open for business.

The advice is always tempting, though, because we know that if we go where they send us and fish the flies they recommend, we'll probably catch some trout. But we also know we'll do it in the company of all the other out-of-towners, and since fly-fishing is a solitary sport, it's hard not to think of other fishermen—collectively, if not individually—as the enemy. We always talk it over out in the parking lot before deciding to go where we knew we'd go all along. The tip we've just gotten may be solid gold, but the best advice you can give either a fisherman or a writer is: Don't do what everyone else does. Avoid clichés.

A few springs ago we were told that the conservancy district was hoarding water in the reservoir and the river below the dam was far too skinny to fish well. Naturally we drove up there anyway. There was no one on the water, and although the river *was* low, midges and Blue-Winged Olive mayflies were boiling off, and trout were dimpling the river as far as you could see in either direction. If you weren't a trout fisherman, you might have held out your hand to see if it was raining.

The conditions looked touchy, so we started out making long casts from our knees with twelve-foot leaders and caught fish. Then we cautiously stood up and continued to catch fish. Finally we waded into the pools where trout rose right under our rod tips as if they either didn't see us or didn't care.

We couldn't figure it out. These fish are no pushovers, and in water this low and clear they should have been as spooky as quail. Maybe it was something in the air. One day after lunch, a red fox—normally a shy animal—sauntered over and started cleaning up dropped potato chips under the tailgate of our pickup while we stood not ten feet away. We wondered if she was rabid, then realized a rabid fox wouldn't eat potato chips in the first place, or trot away when she was done with that coquettish glance over her shoulder. We decided she just shared our taste for salt and grease and was a good-enough judge of character to see we were harmless.

That year the weather held chilly and overcast for days, and the hatches came off between ten and three like clockwork. In that time, we saw only two other parties of fishermen on several miles of river, all locals acting proprietary about the easy fishing. Locals have a certain disdain for out-of-town fishermen. They understand that we do a lot to support the local economy by renting rooms and buying groceries and trout flies, but they'd really rather we just stayed home and mailed in the money. In turn, we tried to seem contrite about having lucked into the big secret, and when someone in town would spot us as fishermen and ask how we were doing, we'd play it cagey and say, "The Fork has been real good lately."

We like to come here in the spring when the weather and stream flow are unpredictable. By late summer and fall the river has settled down, and the hatches come off more or less dependably. The river is crowded with sports then, along with lots of guides who are busy making their nut. The fishing is usually good, but there can be an air of commerce that reminds me of a used-car lot.

In spring the weather can resemble anything from January to June—sometimes on the same day—and the river fluctuates illogically as bureaucrats spin the dials up at the dam. Water is a commodity here, and although fly-fishing is said to bring several million dollars a year into the regional economy, the fishery still gets hind tit when it comes to stream flow. The people in charge may or may not be evil corporate overlords, but it's fair to say that they're interested in rivers only because of the price of water. It's a sad state of affairs, but at certain times of year it does make the place wilder and more vacant.

The following April we were told that they were dumping water for calls downstream, and releases from the dam were bouncing up and down daily to the tune of fifty to seventy-five cubic feet per second, putting off the hatches. In fact, when they bumped them up in midafternoon, the rising flows *did* put off the hatches, but in the hours before that the bugs were there and the trout fed happily. We caught fish for a while and were then left with the prospect of a few slow hours, which is pretty much the standard profile for any day of fishing. None of us is any more philosophical about this than the next guy, but we *have* gotten past the pipe dream of nonstop action.

This last time we stayed at the cheapest motel in town, which isn't much, but the price is right. The place was pretty well booked up. There were a few other fishermen pushing the season, but the rivers weren't in great shape yet, so it was mostly plumbers, roofers, and electricians working on some construction sites down the valley. They were polite but perplexed, wondering how we could afford to be running around in rubber pants instead of working. I guess we're not the kind of people you'd pick out of a crowd as members of the leisure class.

It was early May in a big snowpack year, and they were drawing down the reservoir to make room for the expected heavy runoff, so the river was at about twice the ideal flow for dry-fly fishing. Word in town was that the hatches were off, and your best bet was to cut your losses and go somewhere else. (We always ask, even though we've long since stopped paying attention to the answer.)

Up on the river we spread out and stood there watching for a while. Sometimes before going to work, a cabinetmaker will quizzically heft and stroke an oak plank as though he's never seen a piece of wood before. Likewise, a certain kind of fisherman can watch a run for the longest time before tying on a fly and making a cast. This is a universal ritual of craftsmanship: take a deep breath; don't rush; erase preconceptions. Or maybe they're both reminding themselves that mastery of anything is sometimes a matter of seeing the silver lining in what a less creative thinker would consider a disadvantage. In his book on gambling, Colson Whitehead confessed, "I have a good poker face because I am half dead inside," while the fisherman is thinking, *At least I don't have to try to out-hike the competition, which is impossible anyway on a roadside river.*

But of course the hatches weren't off; they were just thin and sputtering. A few mayflies and midges petered off in waves so sparse you might not notice them if you didn't wait for the occasional minor flurry of rising trout in the soft water along the main current.

I'd forgotten to ask at the fly shop how long the river had been cranked up, but I was guessing at least a few days, since the trout seemed to have gotten over the confusion that's usually caused by these unnaturally sudden bumps in flow. The sky was leaden and the light was gray and flat, but when I got the angle right I began to spot fish against the mottled bottom—first one, then two or three, then a dozen or more. They were lined up in a businesslike way on the inside of the main current in a few feet of water, uniformly cocked a few degrees toward the middle of the river.

I tied on a size-18 Blue-Winged Olive with a smaller midge dry on a dropper and cast to the closest trout. After three or four good drifts, the fish sidled a few feet to the right and took up station closer to deep water—not yet spooked, but beginning to smell a rat.

Then another fish rose a few feet farther up. I covered it with a cast, and when the two flies drifted into the fish's window, it tipped up and confidently ate the Olive as if that's exactly what he'd been waiting for. This was a fat rainbow about ten or eleven inches long, and I played him back toward the tail of the pool to avoid ruining the run.

By fishing carefully up the inside of the current and resting the water between fish, I managed three more trout, one brown, the others rainbows, all in that not-quite-a-foot-long range.

At the top of the run I looked back downstream and saw a splashy rise. It was unlike the quiet sips I'd been fishing to, and it was farther out, just on the edge of the main current. When the rise forms change, it usually means the fish are feeding on something new, and, at least on this river, when they go from quiet to splashy, the small brown caddis flies that hatch in the spring are a good bet. I switched to a size-18 Elk Hair Caddis, cast downstream to where I'd seen the rise, and gave the fly a little upstream twitch as it got close. The fish took; another rainbow that a fisherman of a certain age would describe with the outmoded term "keeper"—that is, nothing to get excited about but big enough not to look pitiful in a frying pan.

One more fish on the caddis fly, and that was it. Either the rise was over or I'd finally worn out the pool. I could see one of my friends in the next run downstream. Over the last hour or so his rod had been bent more often than mine, but his relaxed posture had never changed, which meant he was getting the same pan-sized trout I'd been catching. Another of the guys had been at a pool upstream, alternately casting and sitting on the bank changing flies. I figured he was working on a difficult fish—maybe a big one—and he was sitting at the moment, so I waded up to talk to him.

Sure enough, he pointed out a nice rainbow that I couldn't see at first and then did. It was more colored up than the other fish in the pool and bigger again by half. It might have gone seventeen or eighteen inches.

"What have you tried?" I asked. He listed the same flies I'd have tried, more or less in the order I'd have tried them.

I told him about the caddis fly, and he thought that sounded like a good idea, so I handed him my rod already strung up with the pattern and took his. Then I started wading across the tail of the pool to a small island so I could check out the narrow channel on the other side and the far bank of the run I'd been fishing earlier. I'd gone about ten steps when he called, "Size-18 Pheasant Tail, 7x tippet, one small split shot," so I'd know how his rod was rigged.

At this higher flow the water in the channel was too fast for trout to hold, so I walked down to the tip of the island to look at the softer water downstream. There were no rises, splashy or otherwise, and no bugs on the water that I could see. I stood there for five or ten minutes and was just about to give it up when I spotted a tremendous fish holding just off the main current.

This was one of the bruiser rainbows that still show up here from time to time: deep bodied, brilliantly colored, and well over twenty inches long, maybe as much as twenty-five. Once I spotted him I couldn't imagine how I hadn't seen him in the time I'd been standing there. He was huge, and he was *right there.* All I can think is that after staring at ten-inch trout for several days, this thing was too big to register.

I was on my third cast to this big trout when it occurred to me that a smart fisherman would re-rig with a heavier tippet and a larger fly—at which point the fish took, and it became a moot point.

The trout peeled into the faster current and ran far downstream, where it wallowed and then let itself be reeled back into the V of slow current off the tail of the island. Like many big fish when they're first hooked, this one didn't seem panicked or angry, just puzzled and a little irritated. It hung there in the soft water no more than twenty feet away, held by a tiny little fly, the thinnest possible leader, and a deeply bowed rod. I could see it clearly. It was at least twenty-five inches, maybe longer, and broad across the back: really a stupendous trout. I was staring right into the fish's eyes, and I'd swear it was staring back with a look of bored condescension. I felt equal parts elation and a sense of impending doom and was wondering, *Okay, what now?* when the fish simply shook its head, snapped off the fly, and calmly swam away.

Salmon writer Michael Wigan once described how it feels to lose a big fish: "The suddenly slack tackle is like a telephone line hanging on its cord in the call-box. We feel bereft. The mind floods with a weird sort of cosmic sorrow."

Back at home a friend asked how the trip went, and I said that on my best day I'd managed to eke out only a few small trout and had stupidly lost the one big one.

"So it was a bad day of fishing, then," he said.

I said, "No, it wasn't."

That same spring a friend of mine in his sixties was hiking in to fish a mountain stream in West Virginia when he took a bad fall and broke his ankle. Not twisted, not sprained, but broken. He was alone, a long way from his car, and no one knew where he was, so there was nothing to do but improvise a splint with available materials and start crawling back the way he'd come. He crawled until it got so dark he was afraid he'd crawl right off the trail and end up lost on top of everything else. So he spent the night there—cold, hungry, dehydrated, and in pain—and began crawling again at first light. Later that morning some hikers found him and ran for help.

When the mountain-rescue crew showed up, one of the EMTs

admired the splint, learned that he'd crawled for over a mile, and asked if he had a Special Forces background. When my friend said no, the guy said, "Damn, man, the SEALs missed a bet with you."

My friend had still been on his way to the stream when he fell, so he hadn't had a chance to fish or even tie on a fly, and the doctor said he'd be on crutches for the rest of the season.

Now *that* was a bad day of fishing.

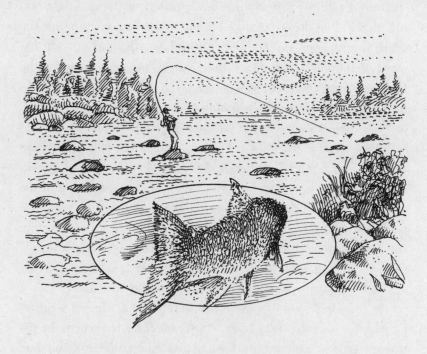

19.

THE LABRADOR EFFECT

I'd flown 2,500 miles across four time zones, leaving Crossroads Lake in Labrador in a fifty-year-old de Havilland Beaver floatplane and arriving in Denver thirty-six hours later in a considerably newer Airbus A319, all on three fitful hours of what you could charitably call sleep. On the drive home from the airport I was bone tired, punch-drunk with culture shock, and beginning to wonder if I was getting too old for this shit, but the next morning, after ten hours' sleep and plenty of coffee, I began to think maybe not. So I got together a pile of dirty clothes that smelled of sweat, fish, wood smoke, and bug dope and asked Susan if she had anything for the wash. She said yes, but she didn't want her girly stuff in with that mess. At the end of every trip there's a precise moment when the spell is broken, and that was it.

This had been my ninth fishing trip to Labrador and my sixth to Three Rivers Lodge in the last thirteen years. I understand what sustains a habitual trip—it's a slippery emotion that falls somewhere between affection and self-interest—but it's less clear what engenders one in the first place. It always starts with good fishing in the simplest terms, but then the more granular details that comprise familiarity—how to gather and brew Labrador tea, or that white-crowned sparrows throw their heads back when they sing like Robert Goulet—begin to accumulate into something like homesickness. Why this happens in one place and not another is anyone's guess.

On the Elk River drainage in British Columbia, where I went repeatedly for almost twenty years, it had something to do with the native west-slope cutthroats, the big bull trout that would now and then eat a fifteen-inch cut right off your leader, and a skilled but maniacal guide known as "Speed Bump," because he once ran over himself with his own car. (Don't ask; it's a long story.) I've heard that this guy has since married and settled down, but at the time he conducted the kind of love life that would have killed a weaker man—or so he claimed.

That trip finally soured with the advent of crowds and reams of expensive new special permits that turned fishing a wild river system into something that resembled filling out your tax return.

On the Valentine National Wildlife Refuge in Nebraska it was the workmanlike largemouth bass, the 270 species of birds that migrated through every year, and the ramshackle fish camp that had been run by the Ballard family as a sideline to their hog farm since the 1950s. Even after ten years we were still newcomers compared to those who'd first fished the place as children, and who were now fishing with *their* children, and in some cases their *grand*children.

That one went south when the Ogallala Aquifer that fed the lakes began to dry up from the effects of too many irrigation wells. The last time we fished Rice Lake it had shrunk to the size of a large puddle, and the flooded timber where the bass used to hide was now behind us on dry land. And then the state decided to cancel the Ballards' lease and bulldoze the old cabins because they weren't up to code and replace them with a slick new campground and RV park. The fishery was dehydrating and the fish camp was being gentrified. It was time to move on.

Nothing lasts forever, and after a while you start waiting for the other shoe to drop. When you find a place that seems unspoiled, it's easy to see yourself as the lone wolf running ahead of the pack into new territory, although in darker moments you suspect that you're simply in the first wave of fun hogs that will eventually use the place up, unless mining, logging, pollution, or climate change do the job first. The days when you could think of the natural world as immutable may well be coming to an end, and regular fishing trips are now like blue jeans: just when they start to get nice and comfortable, the knees blow out. The only alternative to living with regret is to go looking for new water.

When I decided to try Labrador, I found that there weren't a lot of places to choose from (unlike in Alaska, where there's an outfitter on every corner) and that travel to the region was complicated, expensive, and time-consuming. But I'd also heard from people I believed that it was blissfully uncrowded and that the biggest brook trout in the world lived there, so it seemed worth a shot. I've always had a soft spot for brook trout, and up till then the biggest one I'd caught might have weighed a pound if I'd left my thumb on the scale. In Labrador, two- and three-pounders were considered run-of-the-mill, a "nice" fish came in at four or five pounds, and my

181

biggest on that first trip weighed just shy of eight. I guess you could say I saw the light.

So after sniffing around at different lodges for a few seasons, I found a place I liked and settled in to become a regular: that species of fisherman who's as persistent as a stray cat, and for the same reason—because he's getting what he wants. For the cat, it's regular meals and a spot on the couch. For the fisherman, the payoff comes partly in fish and partly from bear-hugging the folks you once only shook hands with. It's important to find people and places far from home that you love. If nothing else, it makes the world seem big and friendly instead of small and mean.

On this last trip, a full complement of eight of us flew into camp on a venerable Otter chartered in the nearest town, 150 miles to the south. It was a crowded flight, with every seat filled, our gear stowed behind cargo netting at the rear of the cabin, and the aisle stacked shoulder high with a week's worth of supplies, ranging "from whisky to ass-wipe," as a dockhand put it. In an emergency, we'd have had better luck trying to kick out a window than climbing over this pile of stuff on the way to the door.

We were the usual odd mix of sports—a couple of borderline but still serviceable geezers, the rest fit enough by varying degrees—and we'd each made this pilgrimage to catch the brook trout that were unimaginable in any other part of the world. Some of us already knew that these fish could induce the kind of hysteria that causes a normally self-possessed fly-fisher to prematurely yank his fly from the jaws of a hog (a phenomenon I've come to think of as the Labrador Effect), and the rest would find out soon enough. On a day when your nerves get the best of you, it's possible to miss more sheer tonnage of brook trout here than you'd seen in your life up till then.

If you learned to love the carefree little brookies sipping mayflies in the creeks and beaver ponds back home, these Labrador brook trout will seem like a separate species. It's not just that they're so much bigger, but that they got that way by eating mice, lemmings, and large sucker minnows. That's what gives them the broad shoulders and the hair trigger you don't recognize in the pretty little fish at home. You naturally bring dry flies, and sometimes they work beautifully, but the more dependable patterns are often the largest available deer-hair rodents and giant, articulated streamers fished on a nearly slack leader to mimic an injured bait fish.

There's an enormous amount of water here in the form of large, sprawling lakes, but you only fish the short riverine channels that string them together at wide intervals, because that's where brook trout congregate. Some days you spend almost as much time traveling by floatplane or canoe as you do fishing. Once you get where you're going, the water is often big and fast, and this is geologically young country, so the rocks haven't yet been worn smooth or shimmed in place with sediment. The bottom is uneven, angular, and teetery, with sudden dark holes. It helps if you're a strong wader, but sometimes you can make up the difference with heroic casting.

The brook trout here are what biologists call "locally common," which means they're either there or they're not, and they're known to travel long distances for no apparent reason. A few years ago a large brook trout was caught and tagged at Fifth Rapids, then was caught the next day thirty miles away, and then a few days later turned up back where he'd started. Why the sixty-mile round-trip in less than a week? No one knows.

So fish are sometimes absent in what are considered the most dependable places, but the flip side is that any of these riffles can be like a good steelhead run that didn't produce yesterday but today is full of fresh, eager fish. And of course, sometimes they're there—stubbornly hugging the bottom—but they refuse to bite. Maybe they fed heavily before you got there and are now full, or maybe they just swam thirty miles and they're tired.

There are noticeable differences among spring, summer, and fall, but on any given day throughout the short season the weather can be warm and sunny, cool and cloudy, cold and breezy, drizzly, rainy, or so windy it blows your hat off and makes casting in any direction but one impossible—or, worse yet, grounds the floatplane and keeps the boats at the dock. Now and then a front rolls through from the north Atlantic pushing low clouds that look like the undersides of battle-ships, and you know your ambitious plans for tomorrow are about to be ambushed by weather.

On warm, calm days in midsummer it's a good idea to wear a bug shirt, a kind of hazmat suit for biting insects, with tightly cinched cuffs and a hood with a mesh face mask. There are blackflies and no-see-ums, countless mosquitoes, an assortment of generic deer flies, and the giant caribou flies known locally as "Cockwallopers." Cockwallopers are like the zombies in all those horror movies: they're slow, dim-witted, and easy enough to kill, but they keep coming, and there are so many of them that they'll eventually get you.

Robin, the lodge owner, likes to say that Labrador is "inhospitable in every possible way," but he says it with the affectionate smile you'd reserve for a big, lovable puppy.

It's all worth it for the big brook trout, but even then it's not for everyone. The odd number-cruncher can land four or five brook trout of a lifetime every day for a week and go home disappointed that there weren't more of them. And there's the headhunter who begins his week in ecstasy over a five-pound fish, but then later finds himself inexplicably dissatisfied with the eight-pound slab he managed to land. Over dinner one evening he asks—as if it has just that moment occurred to him—if bigger brook trout are ever caught. He's told that every once in a great while something in the nine-pound range turns up, and that there are persistent rumors of double-digit fish. For the rest of his time on this incomparable fishery, he acts like a man with an itch he can't quite reach.

That first day in camp, after a big, late breakfast, a couple of us motored down to Vezina Narrows with Anthony, a guide whose thick Newfie accent I've learned to decipher as long as he's not shouting over the noise of the outboard. I landed a couple of brook trout on a dry fly that were on the small side for Labrador—but still three times bigger than anything back home—and an eight-pound lake trout on a deer-hair mouse. It was a good half-day shakedown, and I rode back to the lodge in the canoe watching the endless, stunted forest of spruce and tamarack, thinking about the bone-deep rightness of running water, and looking forward to the meal Frances would be cooking right about then. Unlike some camp cooks who aim for a rustic version of haute cuisine and usually miss, Frances dishes up the kind of plain, good food you want to eat when you're actually hungry.

In the following days we fished some of the usual places, with the mixed results you come to expect. At Third Rapids three big brook trout in a row ate my size-10 Parachute Wulff, even though they hadn't been rising, and the biggest bug on the water was a size-18. Then at Fifth Rapids we couldn't buy a take, even in the fishiest water, and ended up dolefully staring at several large brook trout tucked behind a big rock, agreeing that we were out of options. But then right around the corner at Little Fifth, I hooked and landed a six-and-a-half-pound fish on a big olive streamer. I thought this was a heartbreaker when it took me into the backing in white water, but then the fish wallowed in a big pool until my guide Michel and I managed to stumble down through the willows and loose rocks to net it.

I spent several days fishing with Michel, who describes himself mysteriously as a "French-speaking Spaniard" from a long line of guides and explorers. I even bandaged his thumb one day when he sliced it to the bone on a razor-sharp hatchet while building a fire at lunchtime. It was a bad cut, but with an antiseptic pad, gauze, and adhesive tape, I stopped the bleeding. By way of thanks, he said, "You're like a father to me."

At first glance Michel could be anywhere between a weather-beaten forty and a well-preserved sixty, but it's impossible to guess the age of someone who's worked outside in harsh conditions for decades. Many of these guys start guiding in their teens, and that ageless, leathery squint develops early and lasts for the duration. Michel did tell me that this was his thirty-seventh straight year of guiding fishermen in the summer, hunters in the fall, and snowmobilers in the winter. He said he's home so seldom that when he does drop by he opens the front door, tosses his hat inside, and waits on the porch to see if his wife throws it back out again. "If she does," he said, "I try again the next day."

One afternoon a fisherman had a banana in his lunch, and I offhandedly mentioned to Michel that where I come from, a banana in the boat is considered bad luck. Apparently this superstition hadn't yet made it that far north, and he reasonably asked, "Why?"

"I don't know," I said. "Why is it bad luck to walk under a ladder?"

"Is it?" he asked.

By dinnertime that evening the news had swept the camp like an airborne virus, and I was sorry I'd brought it up. Several of the guides asked me about it, not exactly buying into it but willing to keep an open mind, and Frances asked, "What about my banana bread?" She was clearly worried by the idea that her fabulous baked goods could put a hoodoo on anyone's luck. I seem to remember her actually wringing her hands, but she might just have been drying them on a dish towel.

From my newfound position as an authority on the supernatural properties of fruit, I took a flier and pronounced, "It's only whole bananas. Once they're peeled, mashed, and baked into bread, the curse is broken."

One day we flew out to Indian Rapids with Kevin. He's the camp manager, but still takes days off to guide, especially in the places he likes and knows so well that you'd be at a real disadvantage if he weren't there. At Indian Rapids he'll lead you to a spot that looks like every other place in this wide, nearly featureless channel, and then stand there leaning on his long-handled net. Like the others here, Kev guides in the hands-off style that some don't recognize as a professional paying you the compliment of assuming you know what you're doing. This is especially puzzling to those who are used to the American model, in which the guide all but hooks the fish for you and then hands you the already pulsing rod.

If you ask Kev about a fly he likes, he'll say, "Yes, that's fine." To one he likes less he'll say, "Well, it could work." In this way you end up catching fish on flies you appear to have chosen yourself.

Kev is short, lean, wiry, and pushing seventy, but he regularly out-hikes much younger sports while carrying a large, heavy pack and wades fast water as if he were strolling across a paved parking lot. He and Frances have been married for years, and as a mature couple they now exude the quiet dependability of a surrogate mom and dad, but it's said that when he was younger Kev was fond of drinking and brawling. You'd believe that the old, angry scars on his neck were the result of a bear attack or a chain saw accident, but I'm told they're from a broken bottle in a bar in Halifax, and you should see the other guy.

It's a testament to the amount of water here that after six trips, some longer than the regulation week, there were still places I hadn't seen. One of those was a small, fast, rocky creek that reminded me of the mountain streams in Colorado where a ten-inch brook trout will make your day, except that this one held some really impressive fish.

I tried a dead-drifted dry fly and got nothing. Then I skated a two-inch-long Bomber and got flashes, but no takes. I asked Michel about putting the two tactics together, and he shrugged. (As I said, at least until proven otherwise, these guys are willing to believe that your guess is as good as theirs.) So I tried a size-10 Stimulator on a down and across-current swing.

That did it for a couple of nice ones, including a hook-jawed seven-and-a-half-pound male that took the fly in slow motion along the rocks against the far bank. There was plenty of time for me to pull the fly right out of his mouth, but I didn't, probably because it was late in the trip and my nerves had finally settled down. This fish was heavy enough to have run me down the creek and out into the lake if he'd wanted to, but he chose to fight it out in the pool, where I steered him around boulders and deadfalls with my heart in my throat until Michel got the net under him. He was a big double-handful with an orange belly and white-bordered fins wearing the universal dumbstruck expression of a caught fish. I told myself that brook trout like this will always be here, and maybe they will be, but the physical sensation of setting up on something big, heavy, and intensely alive was already fading as I slipped this one back into the creek.

20.

THE WEST BRANCH

Jim Babb, his guide friend Danny Legere, and I pulled out of Greenville, Maine, with two canoes strapped to the boat rack on Danny's pickup—a twenty-foot Old Town Tripper and a twenty-one-foot Mad River Grand Laker—along with so much gear and provisions it looked like we'd be gone for a month instead of five days. It was raining lightly, and the chilly morning air was almost too thick to breathe. A day earlier I'd flown from the arid high elevation of Colorado into this dense, humid weather, and just as eastern visitors to the Rockies sometimes suffer from altitude sickness, when we westerners approach sea level we can begin to feel like we're drowning in too much atmosphere.

After two hours on the kind of tire-eating gravel roads where logging trucks have the undisputed right of way, we put in at a bridge that crosses the Upper West Branch of the Penobscot River. At first I didn't think the mountain of gear we piled on the bank would fit in the canoes, but Danny had done this hundreds of times, and by following his directions the load went together as neatly as a Rubik's Cube. The Old Town was packed solid to the gunnels and rode low in the water like a barge, while the Mad River had just enough space for Danny in the stern to run the outboard, Jim in the bow seat with a square foot of legroom, and me nestled amidships on a tarp covering a pile of dry firewood. With the Old Town roped on behind, we ducked under the bridge and motored downstream.

For the first few miles the river was shallow, wide, and placid, with no discernable current to give away the shape of the bottom, and Danny followed the main channel from memory. Mixed woods grew right to the water's edge here, with solemn white pines and black spruce punctuated here and there by the surprising reds and golds of oak and birch. The overcast hung just above the treetops, and a misting rain came and went, the droplets not so much falling as floating in the air like gnats. Late September: nights were getting longer and colder, the moose were into their rutting season, and it wasn't much of a stretch to picture all this buried under snow.

The current picked up around Thoreau Island, and the West Branch began to look more like a proper salmon river, with defined channels, tighter bends, and fishy-looking riffles, runs, and pools. There are ten established campsites scattered along this stretch of good water, each with its own rough pine picnic table and outhouse. On this Tuesday morning some spots were already occupied by hard-core regulars Danny knew by name, but there were still some vacancies, and we moved into Smart's Camp, with its small clearing overlooking a pretty confluence pool.

I had two things in mind for this trip: one was to fish with Jim again, and the other was to catch landlocked salmon. Jim and I had first fished together years earlier on a junket to Labrador. I'd known of him before that and had actually met him when he became the editor of a sporting magazine, but I'd recently had to sic a lawyer on the *old* editor in order to get paid for an article and was still sore about it, so I let the moment pass. It wasn't until that Labrador trip that we discovered we fished at the same pace, shared the same sense of what passes for humor among fishermen, and figured out that we were distantly related and began half jokingly calling each other "cousin." Since then we'd traveled and fished together when we could, but Jim is now semiretired (which is sort of like being a little bit pregnant), and his travel budget has shrunk accordingly, so we hadn't seen each other in several years. In the meantime, the phrase "while we still can" had begun to insinuate itself into our fishing plans.

As for landlocked salmon, I'd caught a few on previous trips to Maine—never enough to say I'd really gotten into them, but enough to want to. These fish are favorites in the regions where they're found, but not high on the life lists of fishermen from elsewhere, even though they're genetically identical to the sea-run Atlantic salmon they'll fly all the way to Iceland or Russia to fish for. The catch is landlocks, or "lake salmon," are usually smaller—though not *always*, as local fishermen will point out.

These fish spend their summers and winters in lakes and run up the rivers in the spring to feed, and again in the fall to feed and then spawn. You can troll for them in the summer or ice-fish for them in the winter, but for many it's hard to think of landlocked salmon as anything but river fish. Jim describes them as "Atlantic salmon that bite for reasons you can understand," and in my limited experience that had rung true. The few I'd caught on dry flies and nymphs had been holding in recognizable lies eating aquatic insects and might as well have been brook trout—at least until they were hooked and went airborne.

But this time we fished for them with streamers, and that made them seem more inscrutably salmon-like. Our successes came often enough that week, but always in isolated flurries as the fish lit up for a while and then turned off again depending on the precise but un-fathomable alignment of time, weather, temperature, place, depth, action, and fly pattern that would be familiar to anyone who chases anadromous fish. Trout have their passing moods, but salmon seem prone to something more akin to manic depression: violent one minute, catatonic the next. You can see this tendency mirrored in the streamer patterns. Many that are still in use are approaching a century in age—a whole roster of traditional feather-wings, each with its own origin myth—and even some of the newer ones still share the unlikely color combinations, exotic materials, and Victorian flourishes that are reminiscent of full-dress Atlantic salmon flies, suggesting a fish that often leaves those who try to catch it scratching their heads.

The two canoes' worth of gear made for a comfortable but not overly elaborate camp, with roomy tents, wood-framed canvas cots, a two-burner stove, a reflector oven, and wicked-good suppers pre-pared in advance by Danny's wife, Penny. He bragged that she'd often be in the kitchen at two in the morning rustling up spaghetti sauce and a couple of pies for a trip before working the fly shop in Greenville all day while Danny was off guiding. There's no doubt that fishing guides are an energetic breed, but it's less widely understood that their wives sometimes put them to shame behind the scenes.

There were even some small, propane-fired space heaters that went by the brand name of Mr. Heater, which we thought sounded like someone's pet name for their Glock. You didn't dare leave one of these on all night for fear of waking up shrink-wrapped in your nylon tent, but the nights got into the twenties and I was sleeping in a borrowed thirty-degree bag, so it was an uncommon luxury to warm the tent before bed and again in the morning before getting up. I developed a cushy predawn routine of waking at first light when I heard Danny lighting the Coleman stove, reaching over to flip on Mr. Heater, and then lying there in the sleeping bag until the tent was warm and the coffee was made. Even with bundling up against the morning chill, I could make it from the cot to that first sip of coffee in under three minutes.

Danny had quickly revealed himself to be one of those guides who keeps things simple while at the same time managing to think of everything, so one evening I was surprised to see him struggling to split firewood with a dull ax. This was so out of character that I asked him about it. He explained that the dull ax was for clients who insisted on helping with the camp chores, even though they couldn't really be trusted with a sharp instrument.

"Okay," I said. "Never mind."

I slept beautifully in this camp. The prewarmed tent helped; so did the uncomplicated tiredness that comes after a day of fishing, plus a stomach full of good food and the river music of current a few yards from the tent flap. The only exception was the night two moose started romantically carrying on across the river. I woke up disoriented by the commotion. The bull was grunting, the cow was bleating and moaning, and for an instant I thought I was overhearing a porn film through the thin walls of a cheap motel room. When I figured out what it was, I listened pruriently for a few minutes, wondering if this was foreplay or if they were actually closing the deal, and then promptly fell back to sleep. I thought maybe this soundtrack would trigger a hair-raising erotic dream, but no such luck.

When he was arranging it, Jim had said this trip would put us on some of the best landlocked salmon water in the region at the best time of year, with one of the most experienced guides in the state:

not exactly a guarantee of success, but a really promising proposition. And, in fact, by the time we knocked off for supper that first day out, I'd boated as many landlocked salmon in a few hours as I had in all my previous attempts combined. Danny had all the right streamers, and the fish were up from Chesuncook Lake right on schedule, with a sweet tooth for forage fish. It was a simple case of being in the right place at the right time with a guide good enough to remove the bulk of the guesswork, but I was pretty proud of myself anyway, and the fly rod that can be such a dumb stick some days had begun to feel like a powerful but friendly animal.

I caught some of my salmon on a fly pattern Danny swore me to secrecy about for professional reasons—no one on the river uses it, and he wouldn't mind keeping it that way—while most of the rest came on Black Ghosts, Blue Streaks, and Montreal Whores. (Being from Colorado, I was given a pass on the pronunciation of that last pattern—in the proper Maine dialect, "whore" becomes a two-syllable word pronounced "ho-uh.") But Jim, with his editor's penchant for accuracy, couldn't help pointing out that "a 'banger' is an unpleasant English sausage," while " 'Bangor' is a town in Maine." I stood corrected.

As with any species, the trick with these salmon was the revolving fly du jour combined with some particular subtlety of manipulation. Sometimes it was the down and across-current, tight-line swing you'd use for steelhead or when wet-fly fishing for trout; other times they wanted a retrieve ranging anywhere from a slow pull to the fastest strip imaginable. But the fallback was always the traditional steep, downstream swing with the rod tip jigged up and down to make the fly dart like a minnow in the current. There are endless variations on this, from a constant, deep pumping of the rod to the occasional short lift, always bearing in mind that trying to catch a salmon is like playing with a cat: the rules change without notice, and your problem is often nothing more than a failure of imagination.

These were small, handsome salmon that hit aggressively when they were biting and might as well have been nonexistent when they were off their feed. You could think of them as miniature landlocked ocean fish making the best of things in freshwater, or as a distinct game fish in their own right, on the order of a deluxe trout. Take your pick. They were strong fighters, and every last one I hooked jumped repeatedly, including the occasional five-inch dink I wouldn't have thought would be strong enough to pull the sink-tip line all the way to the surface.

My biggest were in the eighteen- to twenty-inch range—a size that's considered to be a nice-enough fish—but I knew they sometimes came bigger, and one afternoon we talked to a man who, two days earlier, had hooked, played, and lost a salmon he described as "at least twenty-eight inches long and thick as a canoe paddle." He was still wide-eyed when he told the story, amazed that he'd had a close brush with such a fish. He was naturally heartbroken about not landing it, but also saw it as an adventure in possibility, so he'd been fishing with that vision in mind ever since, not really believing he'd hook that same fish or another like it again, but not entirely resigned that he wouldn't, either.

That guy was with a large party camped downstream from us who were following the oldest good advice in salmon fishing—namely, keep a hook in the water and put in your time. I think there were eight of them; their camp looked like a small, homely village, and they otherwise seemed like a pleasantly rough bunch, so I assumed they were locals. Mainers somehow manage to fly-fish without becoming overly impressed with themselves, and, in fact, they say that if you see a snazzy fisherman in Maine, he's probably from Connecticut. These guys had been camped there for so long that the last time Danny was down here, they'd asked him to bring them a newspaper on his next trip in. It takes a long time out fishing to start missing the news of the world.

We were back in camp for lunch one day when a friend of Danny's poled over to say hello in an ancient twenty-foot Gerrish canoe. It's not at all unheard of to see a wooden canoe on the Penobscot, but this venerable old boat was an actual relic from the late 1800s, and as the man leaned casually on his setting pole and talked about the fishing, I went all mushy inside at the sight of a hundred-plus-year-old canoe still in use in the same world where a two-year-old smartphone is obsolete.

E. H. Gerrish isn't exactly a household name, but he was among the first of the boatbuilders who sprang up hereabouts in the 1880s to fill a growing demand for canoes. It was the same commercial boom that produced more recognizable names like Morris, White, Carleton, Kennebec, and Old Town, and continued on into later generations, including our campsite's namesake, Myron Smart. These canoes were modeled after the birch-bark canoes that were built by the people of the Penobscot Nation, who had been living and fishing here since before the Roman Empire. It's said that these craftsmen adopted wood and canvas construction not because it was better than birch bark but because by the late 1800s mature white birch trees big enough to strip for canoes were already getting scarce.

The sports who came up from the cities to fish from these canoes with curmudgeonly Maine guides brought along now-classic eastern bamboo fly rods by makers like Payne, Leonard, and Edwards: rods that were then just good fishing poles, but are now museum pieces too valuable to bring to the river. Fred Thomas's workshop was just downstream in Bangor, where the great F. E. Thomas streamer rods were built within sight of this river.

And then there's the whole Thoreau thing. Henry David Thoreau floated the West Branch twice in the 1850s and wrote about it in his book *The Maine Woods.* He may have understood—or at least hoped, the way writers do—that he'd be remembered, but I wonder if he foresaw that Warren Island would be renamed Thoreau Island in his honor, or that his other stops would become landmarks on the kind of sentimental canoe trips one local outfitter refers to as "soft adventure." Or, for that matter, that he'd spawn an entire tourist industry that draws what are known to some as "Thoreau people" and to others as "earth muffins."

The accumulated bittersweetness of nostalgia seems unavoidable here, and it's easy to sit poking your campfire and imagining a past when the fish were bigger, life was simpler, and everyone was off the grid because there *was* no grid. But it's harder to put a finger on exactly when that would have been. Even by the time Thoreau came along and described this country as "grim and wild," a robust logging industry had already been going on for twenty years—leaving behind that industry's distinctive form of wreckage—and ownership of the so-called wilderness was already largely sewn up. Way back in the 1780s when this region was still part of Massachusetts, most of what would later become the state of Maine was sold off in township-sized parcels to private owners who could do what they wanted with it, and, then as now, one of the things they wanted was to sell off the valuable sawlogs.

Much of the northern Maine woods is now privately owned by a consortium of logging companies, and although the legal and financial arrangements that provide access can seem incomprehensible to an outsider, Jim said it boils down to people being allowed to hunt, fish, paddle, and camp here as a concession to the famously irascible character of Mainers who would hunt, fish, paddle, and camp whether they were allowed to or not, so why fight it? Behind that offhand comment you sense regional pride, as well as generations of hard feelings.

The woods along the West Branch now are the kind of old second-growth forest that looks primordial to a casual observer, but that's a calculated illusion, because the state has negotiated five-hundred-foot-wide easements—called "beauty strips"—along both sides of the river where logging isn't allowed.

When I first learned about that, I wasn't sure what to make of it. The romantic in me wanted a backdrop of absolute wilderness instead of a stage set for recreation, but then, to be really upset about it I'd have had to be more surprised than I am that some things aren't exactly what they appear to be. On the other hand, my practical side found it hard to argue with any compromise that lets an extractive industry stay in business while leaving a wild river intact. If nothing else, it provides both loggers and guides with a livelihood and sidesteps the kind of all-or-nothing fight conservationists usually lose.

I can't say I spent a lot of time brooding about this; the fishing was too good for that, and I also understood that if you chase perfection too far down a rabbit hole, you can end up growing your beard down to your belt buckle and carrying a sign that reads "The End Is Near." Still, the twenty-first-century temptation to peek behind the corporate curtain can be almost irresistible, and on our last evening in camp I *did* think about walking five hundred feet into the woods to see if I'd emerge into a moonscape of clear-cuts. But without actually deciding not to, I never got around to it. I say I'll never get used to the way things have changed, but then I do. I do it every day.

The next day we broke camp and motored back upstream to the put-in. The day after that, Jim and I ate a big breakfast at Auntie M's in Greenville and then hiked down the East Outlet of Moosehead Lake, bushwhacking through the underbrush after the fishermen's trail petered out. The fishing was slow, but we managed a few small salmon, and I landed the fattest, prettiest sixteen-inch brook trout I'd seen in a long time. No fishing trip to Maine would be complete without a brook trout.

21.

COLLECTING A DEBT

Just past the halfway mark on the hundred-mile flight north from
the lodge, we pass from dense spruce forest crowded with lakes
and rivers into more open country approaching the ragged edge of
Arctic tundra. The geography here begins to roll into low, bare hills
that loom up surprisingly under the small, low-flying floatplane, giving us hapless passengers an involuntary sinking feeling. The slopes
look soft with mosses, lichens, forbs, and ground-hugging grasses,
but the bare summits expose high spots in the Canadian Shield: the

three-million-square-mile slab of igneous rock that encircles Hudson Bay like a lopsided horseshoe. It's early July—barely spring here— and there are still patches of snow dirtied by windblown grit to the yellowish brown of old Styrofoam washed up in a river.

We've flown from cool, partly cloudy weather into a chilly drizzle. It's gotten cold enough in the cabin that I've got my fleece vest zipped to the chin, and the mosquitoes and blackflies that snuck in when we boarded have gone into comas. I'm sitting in the rear seat next to the owner of the lodge, and the pitch and volume of the plane's 985-cubic-inch radial engine have made conversation futile, but after we've been in the air for over an hour he leans over and yells in my ear, "Too much coffee!"

I don't get it at first, but then notice he's got an airsickness bag on the seat between us and is struggling to pull down his chest waders from a sitting position. I had to pee in an airsick bag myself once on a long flight and understand this is the kind of operation that requires privacy, so I get very interested in the view out my window. Under a low ceiling and a light rain, the landscape is all stark shades of gray, with no visible horizon in the overcast. Through the power of suggestion I now have to go myself, but I'm pretty sure I can hold out till we land.

When we top the last range of hills the ground drops away abruptly, and there's the lake in the distance. The First Nations people hereabouts say this body of water was formed by a meteorite hitting the ground long ago, but still somehow within their collective memory. I have no reason to doubt that, but to me it doesn't look round like a crater; it's longer than it is wide and is the same apparently random shape as any lake, with the same bays and points you'd see anywhere. On the other hand, I'm told that on a live, green planet with water, weather, plate tectonics, and volcanism, old craters can stretch and sag like an aging face until they become all but unrecognizable.

As I have the three other times I've flown here over the last dozen years, I scan from the air, looking for the rock. There's supposed to be a pyramid-shaped black basalt rock somewhere in or around this lake that's so meaningful to the native inhabitants that they're forbidden to mention it by name, look at it, or even point toward it. So where is it? The best you'll get is a vague toss of the head over one shoulder or the other while you search the impassive face for a hint of either earnestness or a suppressed smile. It's an ongoing struggle to respect the beliefs of others without understanding them, bearing in mind that the details of your own convictions would also sound goofy out of context. But the effort is complicated by the fact that some First Nations people enjoy fucking with white guys who, having been trained by books and movies in which wise natives dole out mystical wisdom to Caucasians, will pretty much swallow anything. As an outsider with only the sketchiest idea of what's going on, I simply nod solemnly and keep my mouth shut. I'll never know for sure, but it's better to be played for a fool than to risk an unintended insult.

This story comes from a nativist type: a guy who knows, observes, and in some sense lives by the old ways even as he tumbles for chain saws, outboards, and Tim Horton's coffee just like the rest of us. I happened to be there the first time the lodge owner met him. He took in the floatplane and our small party of sports in GORE-TEX waders and politely said to my friend, "I'm pleased to meet you, but I'm not happy to see you here."

Fair enough—our history together on this continent has not been a happy one—but in the end, after an hour and a half of rambling conversation that for the longest time seemed to be going nowhere, we got grudging permission to fish. It wasn't entirely clear to me that we *needed* permission, or that this was necessarily the person who could give it, but we got it anyway, possibly because we bothered to ask.

Anyway, I've never seen the rock, but I might not know it if I did see it. I'm naturally looking for a monolith straight out of *The Lord of the Rings*, but since it can't be talked about, no one ever said how big it was. For all I know, it's the size of a coffee table.

The pilot banks over the stretch of lake near the outlet where he plans to land, scanning the surface. He knows it's deep enough here, but on the way in we could see that the bays on the leeward side of the lake were still choked with chunks of ice, and he doesn't want to hit one that might still be bobbing around in open water. For that matter, he doesn't want to hit anything else, either, like a floating log or a swimming caribou or something entirely unexpected. It's precisely the unexpected stuff that will mess you up, which is why the good bush pilots all have a careful streak.

Once the plane is tied up, we form a line from a pontoon to the gravel beach and pass out our minimal gear: a pack and rod case for each of us, plus a shotgun—an ancient Russian single shot that looks like it would make a better club than a firearm. In a way, the gun is a prop designed to make the clients feel safer, but there *are* lots of black bears here, and they have a reputation for being uncharacteristically snarky. Fishermen have been false-charged, and the first time I fished here a large bear came down to the far side of the river and paced back and forth, glowering at us with his head down and his ears back like an angry Rottweiler.

We string up our rods and shoulder our packs and hike a quarter mile down the beach to the outlet and on down the river, leaving the pilot to wait with the plane for the day. This must be the hardest part of a bush pilot's job: waiting alone for hours on some lonesome beach while everyone else is off fishing. Sleeping and reading are the two most common pastimes, but some take short walks—never straying far from the plane—do paperwork, or sit quietly on a log and give a good cigar the undivided attention it deserves. The bush pilots I've met all shared a methodical nature along with this kind of monkish patience. They seem to have learned the lesson my old cat, Bob, spent his life trying to teach me by example—namely, when there's nothing to do, then do nothing wholeheartedly.

This is a scouting trip to see if the fish are in the river yet, and since this isn't the kind of place where you can look up the current conditions on a website, all you can do is mount an expedition and go have a look. The Arctic char that live here spend most of the year in the depths of the lake, where they're out of reach of fly-casters, but they move down into the river to feed on bugs and forage fish through the short summer. It *is* summer, technically, but it doesn't feel like it. The sky is charcoal-gray, and the air temperature is in the low forties, but the steady light rain and stiff downstream breeze drop the wind chill at least another ten degrees. We were hoping for a water temperature of around fifty, but the stream thermometer says thirty-seven. That's not a good sign, but it's not a surprise, either. The late ice in the lake was our first hint that we might be too early.

The river leaves the lake here in a single tongue of wide, smooth current that looks placid but is actually swift enough to knock you down if you don't brace for it. This is big water, with many places where, however deeply you wade and however ferociously you double-haul, your cast falls pitifully short of the distant deep slots where the fish are likely to be podded up. So the established tactic is for the guide to lob a large spoon into the deepest water and retrieve it as fast as the handle on a spinning reel will turn. The fish rarely hit the spoon, but sometimes two or three of them will break out of the school to follow it out of curiosity and let themselves be teased into fly-casting range.

That's if they're there, although in water this cold there's a better than even chance they're not. We'll go through the motions anyway, hoping that a few fish have drifted into the river early, and since we'd like to bring back some char to eat, if the guys with spinning rods happen to hook a fish, we'll keep it. (We all consider ourselves to be fly-fishermen, but we're not unreasonable about it.) The char here tend to be big, so we'll need only two or three. Normally that's not a stretch, but today it could take some doing.

We spread out along the first wide bend, the guide and the lodge owner with the spinning rods, my partner and I with nine-foot, 8-weight rods, sink-tip lines, and streamers. His is a Clouser and mine is a rabbit-fur sculpin, but they're both identically hot pink and white and weighted for extra depth. It's said that if these fish are on the feed, they'll move three feet side to side for a fly, but not so much as six inches up the water column.

I'm standing just upstream of the lodge owner, watching him throw the big red-and-white Daredevle four times farther than I can cast my fly and feeling a little envious. His cast is high and across the wind so that the trailing monofilament describes a graceful, parabolic curve. Once he begins reeling I honk out the longest cast I can manage, give the rig thirty seconds to sink, and then begin my retrieve. I want my fly to be as close to the lure as possible to attract the attention of any char that might be following it, but the wind is troublesome, and I'm trying hard not to cross his line. As one of only four fishermen in who knows how many thousands of square miles, I'd feel really stupid if we got tangled up.

Before too long an element of drudgery creeps in. I'm cold and wet—which is discouraging in its own right—and methodically casting into water that may very well not hold fish, but I have to keep the faith. A retrieved streamer should act like live prey, and if my strips become mechanical or my mind wanders, I'll have lost the spark of intention that could draw a strike. This is almost impossible to explain to someone who doesn't fish, but every angler understands that if you don't retrieve a fly as if it matters, then it no longer matters.

But my mind wanders anyway. Behind us, on river left, is a steep stair-step slope of raw glacial till, where some knee-high wolf willows have gained a foothold. Above that—out of sight from here—is a wide, bare, windy bench, and then a second, final slope to the ridge-top.

Once we're done here, we'll climb that slope and cross the bench to get around a sheer cliff and then climb back down to a place known as Big Eddy: the only named pool on this river. On the far bank are tall, staggered tiers of basalt cliffs that look shiny and coal-black when they're wet, as they are now. Below that, along the water, is a fringe of dense alder and willow punctuated by a few raggedy black spruce trees sticking out like sore thumbs. A dozen house-sized boulders are perched precariously high up on the lip of the ridge. Once this region was under as much as a mile of ice, and when the glaciers melted back, they deposited these rocks that have sat here for thousands of years, looking like they're ready to topple into the river at the slightest provocation. There's the idle, frat-boy impulse to climb up there and push one off just to watch it fall.

I'm in the river thigh-deep and have pretty good footing on the gravel bottom, but I'm still standing in a modified fencer's stance against the insistent current, which gives me an extra-rude nudge from time to time. I've been here long enough for the chill to penetrate my waders, fleece pants, long johns, and fat, ragg wool socks. My feet are going numb, and so are my fingers where they stick out of my wool Millar mitts. My nose is running uncontrollably, and probably turning red. Pretty soon I'll have to wade back to shore and stomp around to try to warm up, but the cold here seems to seep right out of the ground, so it won't be that much of an improvement. On the plus side, this is known as one of the worst places in the region for blackflies—real bug-dope and head-net country—but today the hellish little biting flies are absent.

I catch myself thinking about the lodge a hundred roadless miles to the south. Hot food, hot coffee, woodstoves, cozy bunks: every mental image radiating warmth. It all seems impossibly far away, and it *could* be, with nothing more unlikely than a mechanical problem with the plane or already bad weather that deteriorates just enough that we can't fly back.

There are as many definitions of wilderness as there are people who care, but for me a big part of it is this gnawing sense of the indifference of the weather and the landscape and the idea that as much as I love the gloomy, remote drama of this place, if I don't eventually get out of here, my goose is cooked.

The lodge owner says, "There's a nice fish."

The comment seems so out of context that it doesn't register at first; then I realize he's telling me a big char has followed his spoon and is now in casting range—but where? I haven't been paying attention, so I don't know where the spoon is, and although I just made yet another cast on autopilot, I don't know where my fly is, either. I frantically scan the water in front of me. It's perfectly transparent for the first twenty or thirty feet, but beyond that it's the same opaque gray as the sky and stippled with raindrops. I make the first strip in some time that's lively instead of languid, then two shorter ones, and the fly stops as definitively as if I'd hooked a log.

I make a short, hard set, and the fish bores off back toward the main current, angling downstream. No jumping, wallowing, or headshaking; just a strong, no-nonsense, get-the-hell-out-of-here run that peels off all the rest of my fly line along with some backing. I get two fingers into my reel spool to act as a soft break and begin backing out of the water so I can chase the fish downstream. My legs are stiff enough from the cold that they don't seem entirely under my control, but I manage to get out of the river without falling. I can't believe I've hooked a fish. I'm also painfully aware that I hooked this one by accident while daydreaming, so in some pure-sport sense I probably don't deserve it, but I want it anyway. Of course you naturally want to land every fish you hook, but you want it even more when you've come a long way, frozen your ass off, and were convinced up until ten seconds ago that you were in the process of getting skunked.

And aside from the general principle, I want this fish because I plan to eat it; an atavistic treat we catch-and-release fishermen allow ourselves a few times a year in order to shed all the philosophical posing of the sport and get down to brass tacks for a change. I've eaten lots of fish in lots of places, often as fresh as it comes, but the char from this river are the best I've ever had. I've eaten them several different ways, but I especially like the way the cook at the lodge makes them: chunked up a little bigger than bite-sized, dredged lightly in seasoned flour, quickly deep-fried in hot lard to a crisp golden brown, and served with her homemade tartar sauce. (After a cold, strenuous day, you metabolize these cholesterol-laden calories before they can do you any harm.) The color of the flesh could pass for sockeye salmon, while the taste is closer to brook trout, but it's denser and sweeter than both put together, almost like red meat. Given the cost of getting here and back, these fish constitute the most expensive meals I've ever eaten, but that's somehow beside the point. The point is that if there's one fish in the river, there are more, so a mess of them for dinner suddenly looks more promising.

The fight is tense but unspectacular: a few minutes of gaining and losing, but mostly gaining, until finally the fish is in the net. We whack it on the head and string it up on a forked willow stick, and I stand there on the bank doing a marching-in-place two-step to get the feeling back into my feet while I admire my beautiful fish. It's a big male, around eight pounds, with bluish slate-colored flanks covered with pink spots, pale orange fins, and a faint blush of yellowish orange on his belly, and so deep-bodied and round he almost crosses the line between well-fed health and obesity. Having made the decision far in advance, I have no misgivings at all about killing him. On the contrary, I feel as if the world somehow owed me this fish, and the debt has now been settled.

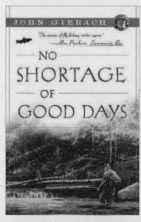
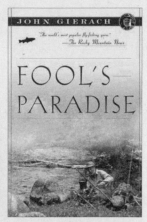
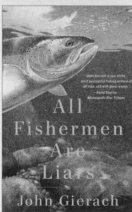